Sheffield and Peak District Walks

30 Favourite Walks

(Volume 2)

By
Stephen Murfitt

Acknowledgements

Copyright. ©Stephen Murfitt 2022

All Rights Reserved. No part of this publication may be reproduced, stored, duplicated, or transmitted in any form or by any means – electronic, photocopy or otherwise without written permission by the publisher or author. Recording of this publication is strictly prohibited.

Printed by Mensa Printers, 323 Abbeydale Rd, Sheffield S7 1FS

Published by Independent Publishing Network

ISBN: 9781800685819

Front Cover Photograph: Ladybower Reservoir

Back Cover Photograph: Bradfield Milepost

Maps & Photographs: Stephen and Andrea Murfitt

Maps are provided only as a guide and are not necessarily to scale. We would advise that anyone using this book also uses a printed map alongside the written instructions.

Disclaimer: The information in this book is given in good faith and is believed to be correct at the time of publication. No responsibility is accepted either by the author or the printer for errors or admissions, or for any loss or injury howsoever caused. Only you can judge your own fitness, competence and experience when undertaking any of the walks.

Sheffield and Peak District Walking Group have created and provided the routes and information for all the walks.

Thanks to Caroline Haynes for all her advice and help with the putting together of this book.

Feedback on this book would be welcome. Please email Stephen Murfitt at sheffieldandpeakdistrictwalks@gmail.com

Foreword

For a good number of years, I have been involved in group walking. First of all, by being a group member, and then for the last 15 years by arranging and leading walks for a number of local groups on a regular basis. Over time, using the walks that I have put together, I have managed to build up a large collection of walks which I have led for these groups, some of them in Sheffield and South Yorkshire, and quite a lot in Derbyshire.

Early in 2021, when the three month lockdown was introduced, that was the end of my group walking for a while, so for something to do with my spare time, I turned my hand to book writing, and produced a book of some of my favourite walks. Never having done anything like this before, it was a very steep learning curve to start with, but a very enjoyable thing to do at the same time.

One thing that proved to be particularly difficult though was choosing which walks to put in the book. In the end, for various reasons, I had to leave a lot of good walks out, and because of this and the advanced interest in the book from walking friends, I decided to call the book Volume 1. This was more out of hope, than any definite plan for a Volume No 2, but as it has turned out, due to Volume 1 going better than I could ever imagined, here we are now with Volume 2!

The format for Volume 2 is exactly the same as Volume 1, and I have only made one small change to how I have put together the walk details, which is as a result of feedback I have received from people who have bought the first book. What people have said is how much they enjoy the information included in each chapter about things which can be seen on the walks. So basically, instead of adding a second photo to some of the walks when there is space to do so, I have included additional interesting information instead.

Anyway, I hope you enjoy reading about my 'new' 30 favourite walks and try some of them out and enjoy them just as much as I do. And if you ever fancy trying one of our group walks, there is information about the types of walks we do, when they normally take place and how to contact us further on in the book. Please also feel free to email to let me know what you think of the book, and if you do decide to join us on a group walk, you'll be made very welcome indeed. Hope to see you soon. Steve.

Contents

Page No.

Walk No 1: Bamford Edge .... 7.25 miles 6
Walk No 2: Dale Dike .... 4.75 miles 11
Walk No 3: Bole Hill Quarry .... 4 miles 17
Walk No 4: Sheffield's Matlocks .... 5 miles 22
Walk No 5: Lathkilldale .... 8.5 miles 27
Walk No 6: Wharncliffe Crags .... 8.5 miles 32
Walk No 7: Grindleford .... 5.25 miles 37
Walk No 8: Parkwood Springs .... 4.25 miles 42
Walk No 9: The Great Ridge .... 9 miles 48
Walk No 10: Wortley Hall .... 7.5 miles 53
Walk No 11: Calver .... 5 miles 59
Walk No 12: Sheffield Lakeland .... 8 miles 64
Walk No 13: Carsington Water .... 8 miles 69
Walk No 14: Birley Edge .... 5.25 miles 73
Walk No 15: Shillito Wood .... 4.75 miles 77
Walk No 16: Victorian Sheffield .... 5.25 miles 81
Walk No 17: White Edge Moor .... 8.5 miles 87
Walk No 18: Limb & Porter Valleys .... 5.25 miles 93
Walk No 19: Ford & Ridgeway. .... 4.75 miles 99
Walk No 20: Ecclesfield .... 4 miles 103
Walk No 21: Edale .... 7.25 miles 107
Walk No 22: Totley Moor .... 5.25 miles 111
Walk No 23: Baslow .... 7.5 miles 117
Walk No 24: Mayfield Valley .... 4 miles 122
Walk No 25: Dove Dale & Ilam Hall .... 8 miles 127
Walk No 26: Hallam Moors .... 5 miles 132
Walk No 27: Bolsterstone .... 8.25 miles 136
Walk No 28: Moorseats Hall .... 4 miles 140
Walk No 29: Crook Hill .... 4.5 miles 144
Walk No 30: Ughill Moor .... 8.5 miles 149

Map Legend

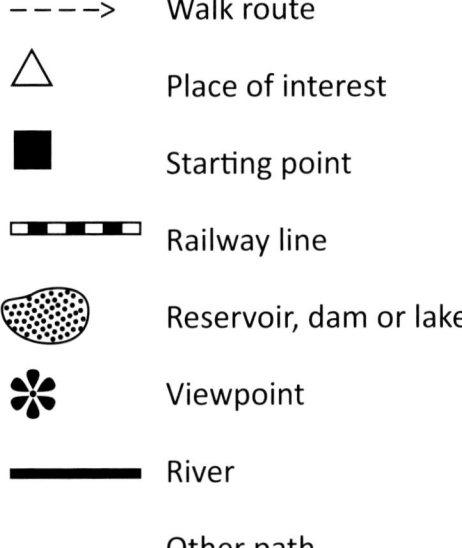

- - - -> Walk route

△ Place of interest

■ Starting point

▭▬▭▬▭ Railway line

Reservoir, dam or lake

✿ Viewpoint

▬▬▬▬ River

──────── Other path

What3Words

What3Words is an app which can be downloaded free to mobile phones and was designed for use by emergency services to locate people who need help and don't know where they are. It works by giving every three square metres in the world it's own unique three words, and is perfect for walkers to find exactly where a walk starts, particularly if there is no postcode. In each chapter of this book, along with the starting point address, are three words which when entered into the app will give directions via Google Maps to the exact starting point.

Walk No 1 : Bamford Edge

7.25 miles /4 hours

Introduction

This is a walk in one of the most popular areas in the Peak District, and has fantastic views from Bamford Edge of not only the Ladybower Reservoir, but also Win Hill, Shatton Moor and the Hope Valley. Starting with a climb up to the Edge, the route then moves on to a delightful section through fields and minor roads in the Outseats part of Hathersage. The return to start is made via the Thornhill Trail, a disused railway line originally used for the sole purpose of getting materials to the site of the Derwent Valley reservoirs. The walk takes place on mainly good paths throughout, although as with any 'Edge' walks, Bamford Edge is very rocky, and can be muddy too.

Looking back at the Ladybower Reservoir from Bamford Edge

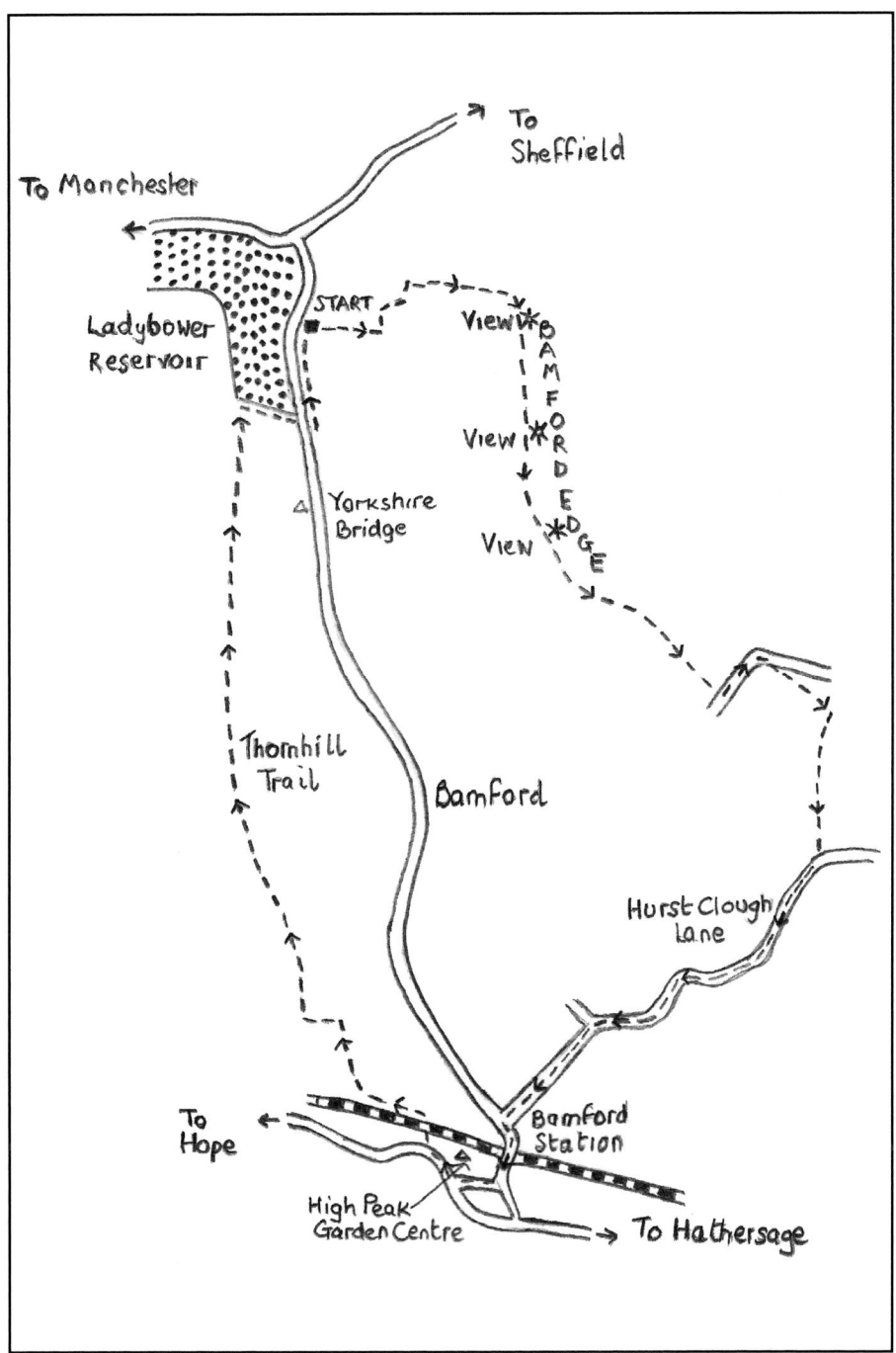

Walk Difficulty

The only really difficult part of this walk is the climb at the start to get on top of Bamford Edge. The total ascent for this section is 125 metres (410 feet) and it is quite steep, but only for about fifteen minutes. The views at the top make the effort worth the while though!

Starting Point

Heatherdene Pay-and-Display car park, A6013, Bamford, S33 0BY. What3Words: **tins.suffice.charities** for the exact start point. There is a limited amount of free parking on the main road on the way to Bamford, just before the Yorkshire Bridge pub.

The Route

High above the entrance to the car park, in the top left corner, take a path leading steeply uphill into woods. Where the path reaches power lines it bends left to follow the lines for a few yards before it bends right to go back into the woods, rising steeply again. Further up, the path bends left with marker posts leading the way towards the corner of a wall. Round the corner, go over a stile and then stay next to the wall on the right for about fifteen yards as the path goes up a banking, before it bends sharp left to carry on uphill through moorland.

At the top, at a junction of grass paths, go right to follow the edge for about three quarters of a mile with extensive views over the Hope Valley all the way. There are various paths leading off this path, but by keeping on the wide path which stays fairly closely to the edge, eventually a fork is reached at the side of a marker post.

Go left, then after 25 yards at a 'T' junction go right. After a small climb a higher ridge is reached. The path stays on the ridge for a short while, then starts to descend. At a fork stay right and carry on down to the road. Turn left on to the road and stay on it as it bends to the right and starts to climb. Half way up the hill, just after passing a few trees, go over a stile on the right on to path which cuts across a banking, with trees to the right.

Where the path ends at a signpost, double back right and after a few yards find a stile in a wall on the left. Over the stile the path carries on downhill through a number of fields keeping in the same direction. After passing a group of houses to the right, and then a pond on the left, the path reaches Hurst Clough Lane.

Turn right and walk down this quiet lane. After 250 yards, at the entrance to Nether Hurst farm on the left, there is the choice of either carrying on down the lane, or going a few yards down the drive to take a path on the right which enters a field and carries on down the hill, tracking the lane for two fields. There is a more open view from the field. Either way, the field path comes out on to the lane further down.

At this point turn right on to a narrow tarmacced lane. After several bends, and almost half a mile the lane reaches a road junction. Go left on to Saltergate Lane and stay on this road until it reaches the main road. Go left to cross the railway bridge then cross the road to a road on the right named Mytham Bridge.

At the bottom of Mytham Bridge turn right to walk along the main road. Immediately after the garden centre take a signposted path on the right and go through a gate on to a path which further on goes through a tunnel under a railway line. At the other side take a path immediately to the left which leads into a field.

Stay to the left border of the field and leave the field in the top left corner on to a track with a big house opposite. Turn left here and ignoring a path to the right, go past a small parking area to take the Thornhill Trail on the right. The Trail climbs steadily uphill for almost two miles to reach the Ladybower Reservoir.

At one point the Trail crosses a road, and just before it reaches the reservoir it is joined by a service road coming up from the right. At the dam wall, go right to walk along the edge of the dam, with views to the left. At the other side, cross the road and take a path which goes up steps before it turns left to return to the car park.

Look out for…..

Hurst Clough Lane which is an old packhorse route where ponies laden with panniers full of salt from Cheshire headed through Bamford and then across country toward Sheffield. It is thought that this route was in fact used even earlier by the Romans on their way to Stanage Edge, from where they headed eastwards on the Long Causeway to their fort at Templeborough at Rotherham.

Thornhill Trail which dates back to the turn of the 20th century when a seven mile stretch of railway was laid from Bamford to aid in the building of Derwent and Howden dams. The line was completed in 1903 and was in use for 13 years during which time it transported more than a million tons of stone from Bole Hill Quarry to the work site. At the end of the line an entire village, known as 'Tin Town', was constructed at Birchinlee for the navvies and their families. It had a hospital, school, post office, pub, shops and railway station but once the dams had been completed, the settlement was dismantled. The tracks were removed in 1916, but then re-laid in 1935 for the building of the Ladybower Reservoir, which was completed in 1943.

Dog Suitability

This is a good walk for dogs, as there are very few sheep on Bamford Edge, and the Thornhill Trail is a great path for dogs to be off lead, apart from where it meets the two roads.

Refreshments

High Peak Garden Centre on Hope Road is a great place to have a cuppa, and the popular Yorkshire Bridge pub is very close to the start/end of the walk. There is also the Ladybower Inn not far away, and the Anglers Rest in Bamford.

Walk No 2 : Dale Dike

4.75 miles / 2.25 hours

Introduction

The walk takes place in both Sheffield and the Peak District and passes through some lovely countryside in the Bradfield area. There are great views on this walk from Blindside Lane across Bradfield Dale and over to Margery Hill in the distance, and there are also some lovely woods to walk through on both sides of the reservoir. Dale Dike reservoir is an iconic place in the area to visit, most famous for the Great Sheffield Flood of 1864.

Dale Dike viewed from above

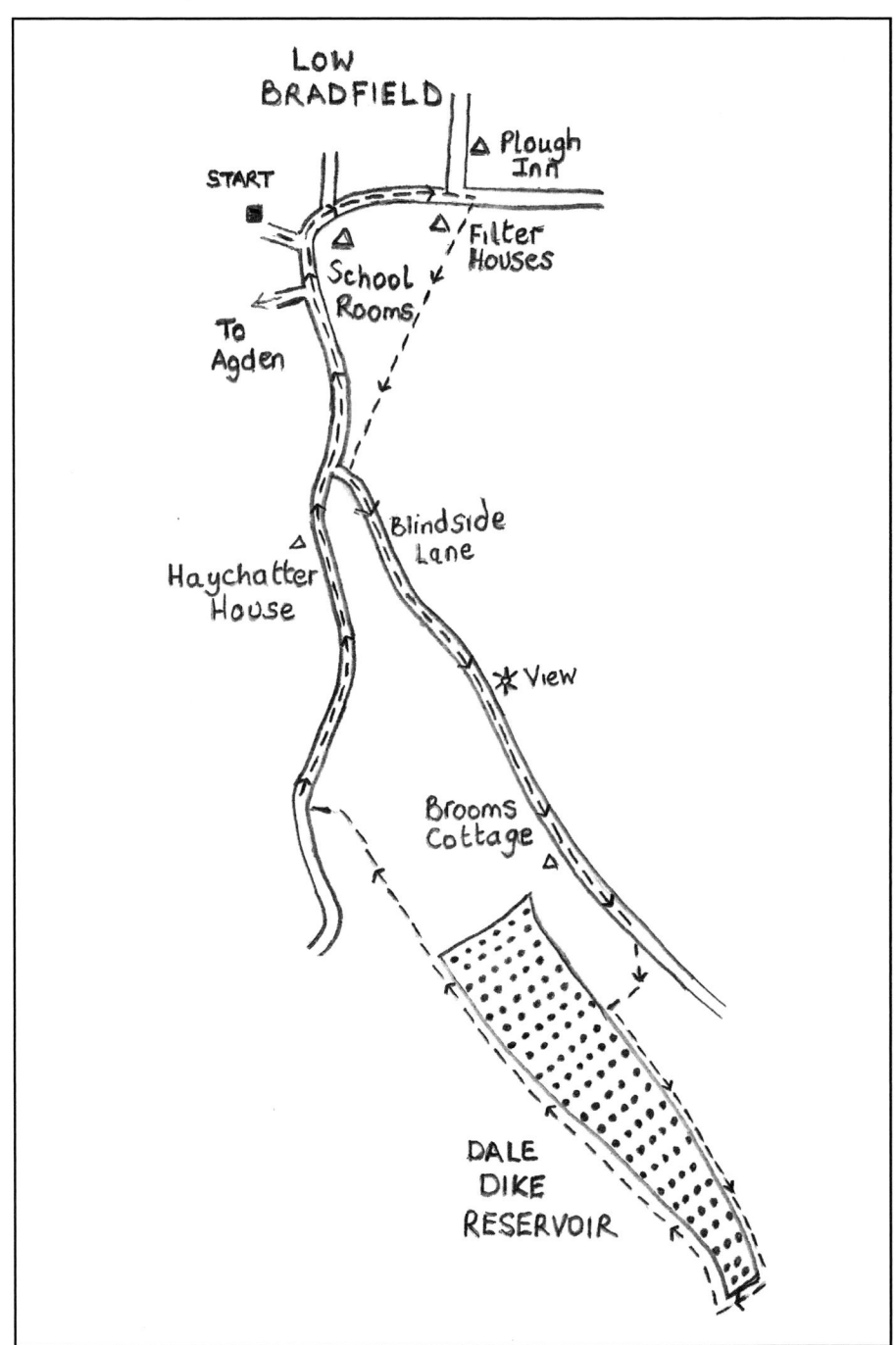

Walk Difficulty

This is a fairly easy 4 ¾ mile walk although there is a strenuous 15-minute climb on the outward leg, and a few difficult stiles too. Expect the reservoir paths to be muddy in winter and after heavy rain.

Starting Point

The Sands Car Park, Low Bradfield, Sheffield S6 6LA. What3Words: **wages.moment.stove** for the car park.

The Route

From the car park, return to the road entrance and turn left on to Fair House Lane. Walk along the road as it becomes Mill Lee Road and bends right and starts to climb uphill. Just past the old Filter Houses turn right on to a track which after a few minutes passes cottages on the right and enters woods. Out of the woods into a field, fork right to head towards a stile at the end of the field. Over the stile turn left on to Blindside Lane. Carry on up the hill, which is steep in parts, for about ¾ mile. About 300 yards after passing Brooms Cottage take a path right into woods.

After 200 yards take a signposted path right, on to an old, enclosed lane which leads down to the reservoir. Over the stile turn left to walk half a mile alongside the reservoir to its end. As the path is joined by a wall on the left, ignore a stile over the wall and stay on the path as it bends right to head towards a stream. Approaching two bridges, take the right one to walk back along the opposite side of the reservoir.

This path stays next to the reservoir for a mile until it reaches the dam wall. After going through a gate on the left take a Water Authority track opposite. The track leads away from the reservoir to climb up to Dale Road. Turn right on to Dale Road to walk along the road to return to the start.

Look out for…..

School Rooms. This restaurant was once Bradfield Junior and Infant school which was built in 1867 to replace a school on a different site in the village which was washed away in the Great Sheffield Flood of 1864. The school closed in 1985 with the 32 scholars being transferred to nearby Dungworth school.

Bradfield Water Filtration Works. The former water board houses filtered water from the Agden, Dale Dike and Strines reservoirs in Bradfield Dale. The filter houses were built in 1913 and in 1930 they became the first buildings in the village to have a telephone installed. The buildings were taken out of use in 1994 and remained empty until 2021 when work commenced to convert the buildings into twenty one dwellings.

The Plough Inn, originally built as a farmhouse, was listed as a beerhouse in the 1841 census and officially listed by the brewery in 1847. The archway was blocked in during the 1960s when alterations took place; it was previously used to take cattle into the auction yard at the rear of the building.

Brooms Cottage. On the 1861 Census a building here is also described as a "Beerhouse", and no doubt obtained an alcohol licence to serve the reservoir construction workers.

Haychatter House dates from the late 1500s and was a farm building for several hundred years. When the reservoirs were built in the dale during the 1860s the farm became a public house serving the large number of navvies who arrived to do the construction work. Initially called the Reservoir Inn and then the Haychatter Inn, the pub closed in 2003. In the 1980's it was used for just one episode of Last of the Summer Wine, although the programme makers stayed in the area for a week, filming other sites in the area for additional scenes.

Dale Dike Reservoir. The Great Sheffield Flood of 1864 occurred on the night of March 11th/12th shortly before midnight. A quarryman who lived nearby discovered a crack in the dam wall earlier that afternoon. The alarm was raised, and a messenger despatched on horseback to summon the Chief Engineer, John Gunson from his home on Division Street, Sheffield. On the way into Sheffield the messenger stopped at Damflask village for saddle repairs, and he mentioned to the saddler about the impending disaster. Later that evening, as Gunson approached Damflask and Bradfield Villages he could see people moving about in the darkness with their possessions etc. making for higher ground as word of the leak had quickly spread. At Dale Dike the Chief Engineer used various means to try and reduce the amount of water inside the reservoir, to no avail.

In the early hours of the 12th, the wall subsequently gave way releasing six hundred million gallons of water into the valley. Over 240 people died in the flood, as the water raced through the valley, destroying homes, bridges, factories and anything else in its wake. The devastation continued not only in the Loxley Valley, but also as the Loxley joined the River Don along its course to Sheffield and beyond. A cow was said to have been seen floating in the Don as far away as Doncaster. Damflask village was completely destroyed and Damflask reservoir was built on its site in 1867. Dale Dike reservoir was re-built in 1875, but further up the valley this time.

Dog Suitability

A good walk for dogs this one, with them being able to be safely off-lead for more than half the walk, and just one small field where there may be farm animals.

Refreshments

Plenty of choice in Bradfield including The School Rooms, Bradfield Post Office and The Plough. The Horns Inn at High Bradfield, and the Nags Head at Loxley are nearby too.

Langlands

More than just a Garden Centre

EST. 1955

VISIT LANGLANDS

LOXLEY SHEFFIELD

Yorkshire's Premier Garden Centres

Langlands Garden Centre Loxley is located in the idyllic setting of the Peak District with lush rolling hills and beautiful scenery. Langlands is a family run business with two additional sites in Yorkshire and is renowned for its outstanding reputation.

HOW TO FIND US:

West Lane
Loxley
Sheffield
South Yorkshire
S6 6SN

📞 Call: 0114 285 1487
✉ Email: sheffield.sales@langlandsgardencentre.co.uk

WE ARE:
- Dog Friendly ✓
- Walker friendly ✓

FACILITIES:
- Toilets
- P Parking
- Cafe

ALSO FIND US IN:

Whinmoor, Leeds, LS15 4NF | Shiptonthorpe, York, YO43 3PN
Call: 0113 273 1949 | Call: 01430 873426

Walk No 3 : Bole Hill Quarry

4 miles / 2.25 hours

Introduction

This is a lovely, wooded walk in the Upper Padley area which as it's highlight showcases Bole Hill Quarry with its interesting history. Before that, leaving from Grindleford station the walk heads through Upper Padley and Gorsey Bank Wood on the way to the halfway point at Hathersage Booths. From there, after cutting through Whim Plantation, the route passes abandoned mill buildings below Millstone Edge before entering the Bole Hill area. The approach to Bole Hill Quarry is made along a delightful grassy path through silver birch trees, and then after leaving the quarry the return to the start is made via the path down from Padley Gorge.

Below Millstone Edge

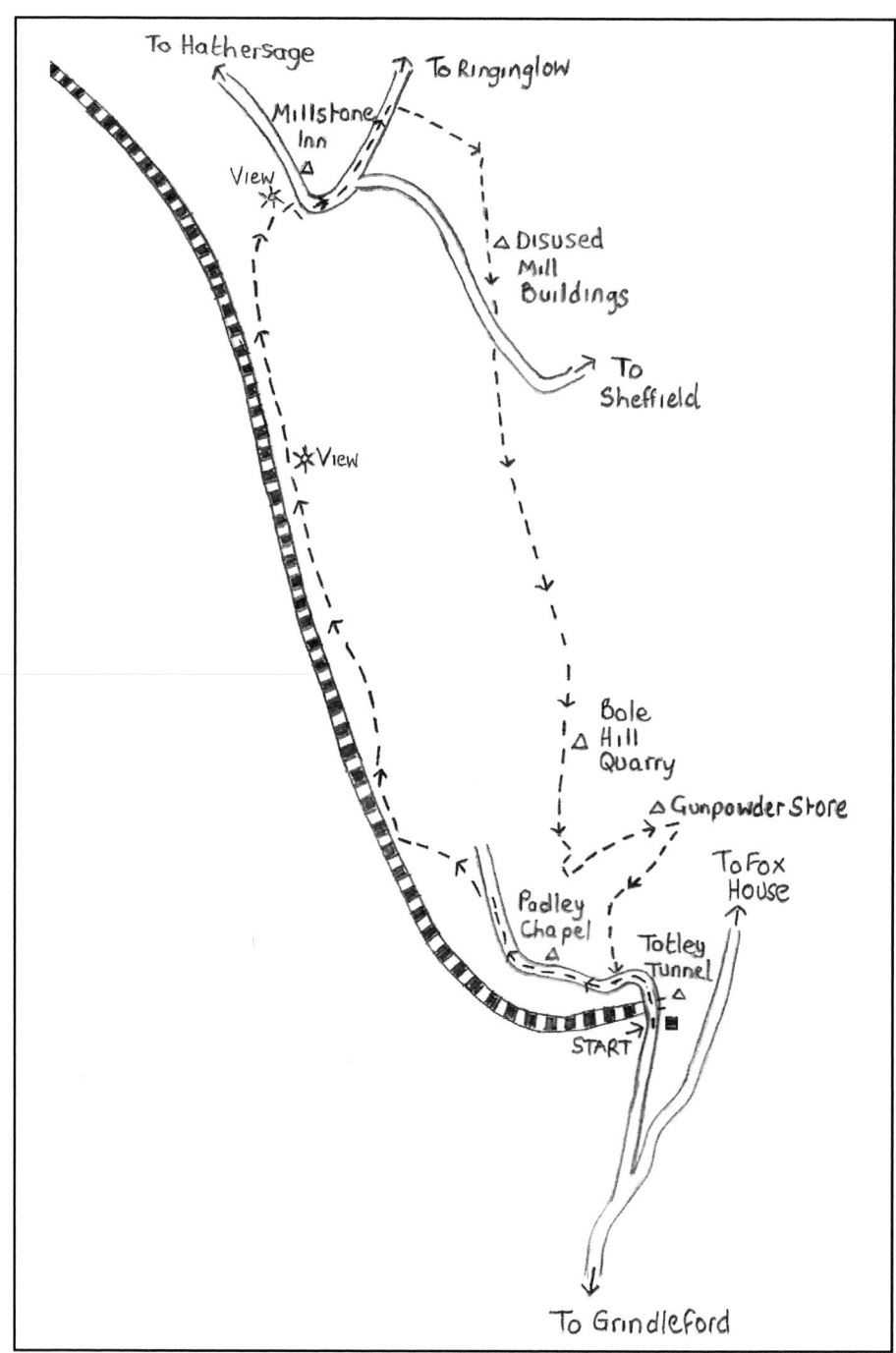

Walk Difficulty

This is quite an easy walk which takes place on mainly good paths. There are sections where there may be mud and standing water, and there is just one short incline, and a slightly tricky downhill section.

Starting Point

Grindleford Station café, Upper Padley, Grindleford, S32 2JA. What3Words: **factor.almost.drill**

The Route

Facing the café turn left to cross the railway bridge and stay on the road which leads through Upper Padley. After a look at Padley Chapel on the right, go through a gate next to a cattle grid and then after passing three houses on the left go through another gate in front. A few yards further on, take a grass path on the left. After going through a gate the path reaches a railway bridge. Take a path right before the bridge to enter woods. This path stays in the woods keeping roughly in the same direction, and just above the railway line. At one point there is a gate in a wall on the right leading into a field. Ignore this and carry on to pass a house on the left in an open area.

After admiring the views towards Hathersage, cross the driveway to the house to head towards more woods. After 30 yards ignore a path left which goes under the railway to enter the woods through a gate in the corner. Keep in the same direction with a broken wall on the left to go through another gate with a complete wall now on the left. Go past a gap in the wall and further on at a footpath sign head uphill, again with a wall on the left.

The path soon reaches a junction of tracks. Go straight across to carry on in the same direction uphill. Higher up, the track meets another track coming up from the left. Join this track as it immediately bends left then straightens to reach Hathersage Road next to the Millstone Inn car park. Turn right to walk along the main road for about 250 yards then cross to take a minor road on the left, walking along it on the right side of the road for about 400 yards.

Just before the woods on the right end, take a path into the woods and stay close to the wall on the left as it gently climbs to reach and go through a wall ahead. Carry on forward for a few yards then at a path 'T' junction go right and keep on this path as it passes disused mill buildings to reach the main road again. Cross the road to go through a gate on to a grass track which further on goes slight right through silver birch trees for 2/3 of a mile with Bole Hill Quarry on the left for most of the way.

At the point where the trees end there are drops to both sides. Between here and Padley there are a number of different paths which all lead to either Padley Gorge or Upper Padley, and any of them can be taken and as long as they lead downhill, one or other of the Padley's will be reached before too long! The route chosen for this walk is as follows: - as the quarry area ends and the path bends slightly right with the drops either side, carry straight on through bracken on a path which leads through a difficult downhill section to reach a footpath 'T'.

Go left here and after 75 yards take a minor path right opposite a gate, which again leads downhill to pass an old building on the left which was a gunpowder store for Bole Hill Quarry. Just after this, the path reaches the main path which leads up and down Padley Gorge. Turn right to carry on downhill on a path which quickly becomes a road through houses. At the bottom of the hill turn left to return to the start.

Look out for…..

Totley Tunnel which is 3.5 miles long and took 11 years to build. Because of the damp conditions, there were outbreaks of typhoid, diphtheria, smallpox and scarlet fever amongst the workforce, with the workers often living twenty to thirty in a house. Working 12 hour shifts, as soon as one man got out of bed, another would take his place, and there was little in the way of washing or sanitary facilities.

Padley Chapel is the remains of Padley Manor, built in 14c and 15c. In 1588 two Catholic priests, Robert Ludlam and Nicholas Garlick were taken from the house and hung, drawn and quartered and their remains stuck on poles in Derby city centre. Their crime was to be Catholics and not Protestants.

Disused Mill Buildings The buildings below Millstone Edge were used as site offices, working sheds and a gunpowder store. Life expectancy of a millstone maker in the 19th century was 40-45 years. Silicosis was a common problem caused by dust from working in the sheds.

Bolehill Quarry the early 1900's was known as a 'super quarry'. Before this though, millstones had been produced in the area since at least the 13th century. The eastern edges of Millstone, Burbage and Stanage were all extensively quarried and Bole Hill was chosen for quarrying due to the quality of the rock there. Millstones, grindstones and crushing stones were made here for over 600 years. In medieval times the local stone was used for millstones for grinding flour, but when the move to white bread came, gritstone fell out of favour due to it making the flour grey. From then on, the stones were used for industrial grinding. Eventually this market collapsed due to cheaper imports from France and the quarry was abandoned almost overnight. In 1901 the quarry was given a new lease though when it was decided that Bolehill was the best place to obtain stone for the construction of the Howden and Derwent dams. Derwent Valley Water Board purchased 52 acres of land and began to remove stone from the quarry face, which was 1,200 yards long, and was estimated to contain 2.4 million tons of top grade building stone. Half of this stone was removed in the seven and a half years that it was worked with at one point, over 400 people working in the quarry.

Millstones. When Bole Hill quarry was almost abandoned overnight the pulp-stones seen there today were left in-situ. They were due to be exported to Scandinavia for use in crushing wood into pulp for the paper industry.

Dog Suitability

This is a great walk for dog owners to have their dogs off-lead. A good three miles of the walk is on woodland paths which are perfect for pooches!

Refreshments

The café at Grindleford Station has a great reputation for serving wholesome food, and there is also a nice local café and shop at Grindleford church. Not far away are also the Millstone Inn and the Fox House.

Walk No 4 : Sheffield's Matlocks

5 miles / 2.5 hours

Introduction

This walk takes place in the lower part of the Loxley Valley and passes through an area named Little Matlock in the 1800's by a local clergyman who loved Matlock in Derbyshire. Little Matlock is now more commonly known as Low Matlock in the valley bottom, and High Matlock high up above, with Little Matlock Wood being between the two. For this walk, the route follows the River Loxley for the first section, where there is evidence all along the river of the effect the Industrial Revolution had in the area, along currently with some 20c factory dereliction. After passing through Low Matlock, a path through the ancient woodland of Beacon Wood is taken, followed by an old packhorse route called Acorn Hill for the climb up to High Matlock. Here, there is more early 19c history from what was the Robin Hood pub, and the area round it, followed by some road walking to return to the start.

Water wheel on the site of an early 18c Corn Mill at Malin Bridge.

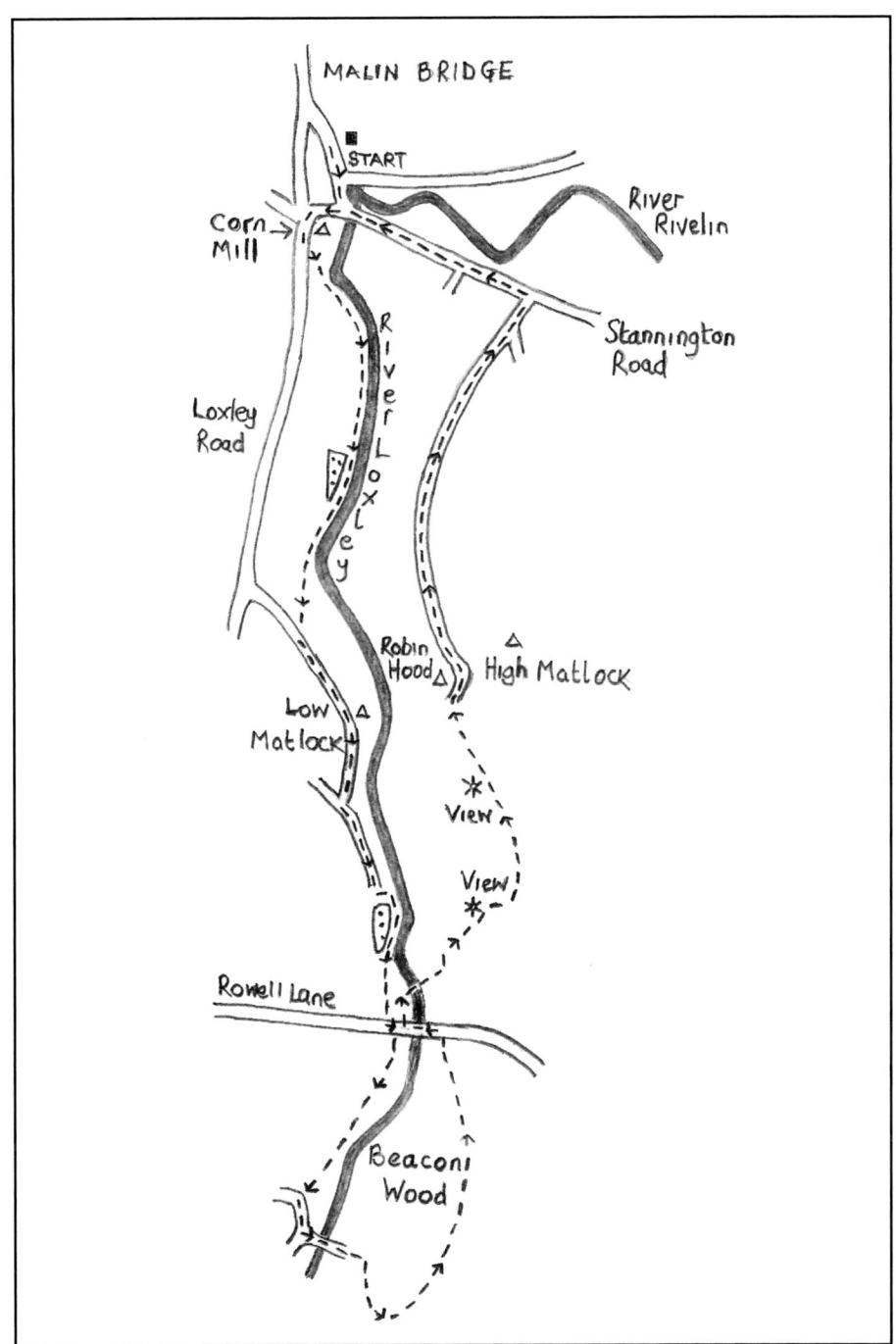

Walk Difficulty

On mainly good paths, this is a fairly easy walk with just one steep 10-15 minute hill climb and not much else in the way of challenges to worry about, apart from the usual mud in winter and after heavy rain.

Starting Point:

Malin Bridge Park and Ride Car Park, 178 Holme Lane, Sheffield S6 4JR. What3Words: **smug.assist.pile**

The Route

Leave the car park by turning left on to Holme Lane, staying on the left side of the road. Cross Rivelin Valley Road, and then Stannington Road as the road bends right to pass the site of the old corn mill and becomes Loxley Road. Stay on Loxley Road as it bends left, then after about 100 yards take the signposted path on the left next to a small car works, to head up Loxley Valley. After passing a retirement home keep to the left of a pond to stay next to the river. The path quickly leads to some steps and at the top of the steps a cross path. Turn left and walk on to Low Matlock Lane.

Turn left along this old track and stay on it for half a mile, passing through Low Matlock to reach Black Lane. Turn left to walk along Black Lane for a quarter of a mile, then at cottages straight ahead take a path on the left which goes round the cottages with the river on the left again. After a third of a mile when the path reaches Rowell Lane, cross the road, turn left, then after a few yards take the first path right to carry on up the valley with the river on the left, and a water channel on the right.

In a quarter of a mile, on reaching an old service road for the industrial estate, turn left and keep to the left-hand side of the road as it bends left to cross a bridge. With industrial buildings and yards on both sides go straight forward towards a row of terraced houses. Keep to the left of these houses to take an unsignposted path which goes round the back of the houses, bending first right, then left as it climbs up into Beacon Wood. Ignore an immediate path right, then after a minute or two at a fork go left to stay lower down in the woods. Eventually this path reaches steps to leave the woods and reach Rowell Lane again.

Cross the road, turn left, then after crossing the river, take the first path right. The path soon bends right to cross the river again to reach concrete steps leading up hill. Go up the steps and where the concrete ones end, and stone steps carry on, take a path on the left. This partly paved path has a wall on the right, and is the start of Acorn Hill.

After a minute or two the path leads into a field. At a second field the path goes left, then after a few yards it bends right to go uphill and into trees. At the top of the hill the path reaches a road. Next to where this path comes out is another path on the left which enters back into the same scrubland area. Take this path which immediately turns right to stay close to the road. Ignore a path right after a couple of minutes leading back to the road, and another right path further on and stay on this path which has steep drops to the left, and houses to the right.

After a quarter of a mile the path becomes a service road for a short way before it becomes a path again and leads to the old Robin Hood pub at High Matlock. Passing to the right of the pub stay on Greaves Lane as it starts to go downhill, as it first joins Myers Grove Lane and then further on, Wood Lane to finally reach Stannington Road. Turn left to go downhill to return to Malin Bridge and the starting point.

Look out for…..

Malin Bridge Corn Mill. There has been a mill on this site since at least 1739, but the present building was built after the Great Flood of 1864. Originally a grinding mill, it was converted to a corn mill around 1915 and operated until 1956. It was converted to housing in 2008 and became Grade II listed.

Beacon Wood has a varied history. A small number of derelict outbuildings in the wood are the remains of Military buildings, which accompanied an anti-aircraft gun used in WW2. The lower slopes of the wood show evidence that it has been used for over 400 years - supplying timber for building, fencing and ship construction.

Low Matlock was hugely affected by the Dale Dike dam disaster in 1864. It was at this point that the flood came down in all its fury, sweeping everything before it, and spreading out into the valley at a point where the River Loxley is at its narrowest. Bridges were washed completely away, trees were torn up by their roots, walls knocked down, and fields submerged beneath water and mud. Tilt and rolling mills were also completely destroyed; heavy masses of iron and machinery were torn from their places, broken into fragments, and scattered. Many lives were lost here, including a number of children.

High Matlock. A gannister and coal mine existed here up to the 1960's. A narrow gauge track ran down the slope and was used to carry the ganister and coal up the hill. Track remains can still be seen on the hill.

Robin Hood Inn. Around 1800, the Reverend Thomas Halliday, minister and entrepreneur, was so struck by the beauty and similarity to Matlock in Derbyshire of a spot along the River Loxley, that he set out to transform it into Little Matlock. Halliday built a house on the hillside, one half of which was from the start used as a pub, the Rock Inn. In time, the pub was re-named The Robin Hood and its claim to fame was that it was the only pub in the country with a beer cellar carved out of natural rock.

Dog Suitability

This is an excellent walk for dogs. There are animals in adjacent fields through the valley, but well-behaved dogs can safely be off-lead here apart from some short road sections. Beacon Wood is a safe place to walk dogs, as is the climb up Acorn Hill and the stretch across to the old Robin Hood pub. From there, it's road walking back to the start.

Refreshments

There is nowhere on the route to obtain refreshments, however there are numerous takeaways at Malin Bridge, the Malin Bridge pub which serves food, and The Anvil on Stannington Road which is drinks only. There are many more pubs and cafes at Hillsborough, and the Rivelin Park café not far away as well.

Walk No 5 : Lathkill Dale

8.5 miles /4.5 hours

Introduction

Lathkilldale is one of the loveliest of the Derbyshire Dales, and this circular walk covers the first three miles of the dale, from the village of Monyash. With the steep, almost vertical sides higher up in the dale, and the cliff faces, it is an amazing place to walk. It is also fairly unique too, with the River Lathkill disappearing underground during dry weather, and the very rare Jacob's Ladder orchid in abundance on its slopes in summer. After leaving the dale, there's a climb up to Long Rake followed by a pleasant walk through farmland, and along old packhorse routes and through Cales Dale to return back to the start.

Trout breeding pools on the River Lathkill

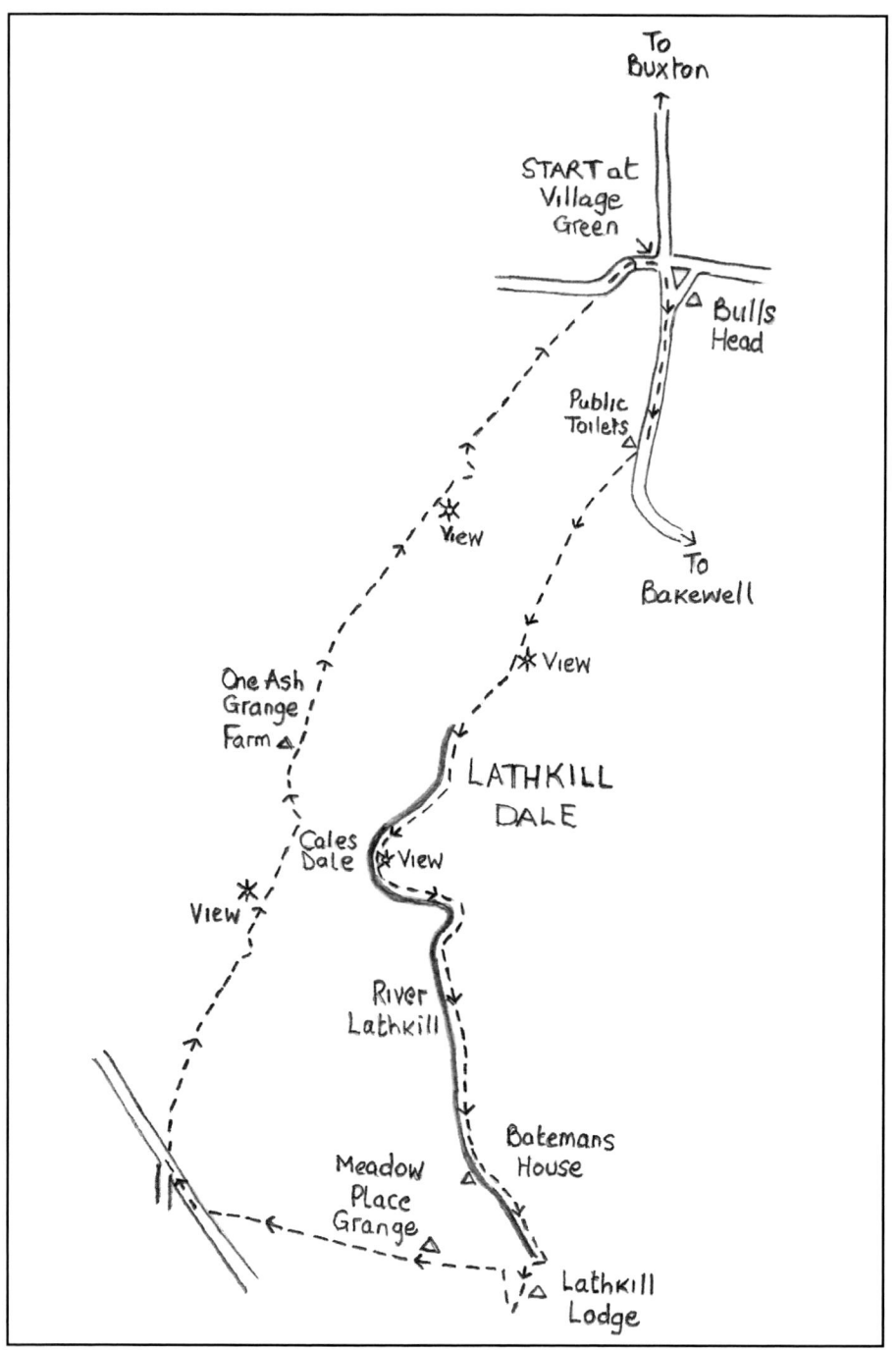

Walk Difficulty

Although this isn't a very strenuous walk, there are some difficult sections throughout. Parts of the walk down the dale are extremely rocky as the path cuts its way through boulders, then there's a stiff climb to get up to Long Rake. After this, there's a tricky path down into Cales Dale, and lots of stiles to tackle whilst crossing the farm fields.

Starting Point

The village green in the centre of Monyash. Postcode for the Bulls Head is DE45 1JH. What3Words: **loom.odds.boot**

The Route

From the village green, head along the road in the Bakewell direction, and as the road leaves the houses downhill, take a path right next to public toilets. This path goes through the Lathkilldale Gorge and at the start the path is a wide grassy track, but pretty soon it becomes rocky, and quite narrow. Before not too long though the route opens up to reveal fantastic views of the steep-sided dale. Stay on this path through Lathkilldale for just over 3 miles to reach a bridge at Lathkill Lodge, the first house to be seen on this path.

Just before reaching the lodge, look for an arched bridge on the right crossing the river. It is worth crossing the bridge here to look at old mine workings on the other side. Meanwhile, at Lathkill Lodge, cross the bridge over the river onto a path which climbs through trees first by going left, and then by doubling right. At a gate at the top, cross a field to reach a large farm, Meadow Place Grange.

Go through the farmyard following various signposts, ignoring a stile left to go over a stile straight ahead on to a track between walls. Over another stile, ignore the path left to go slightly right with a wall on the right. The path soon leaves the wall and becomes a little feint as it heads half right from the wall. If the path cannot be seen clearly look towards the far side of the field for a stile in a wall and head for it. Over the stile go through two more fields heading in the same direction for around half a mile to reach a road.

Turn right and walk up the road for about 10 minutes to take a path right, opposite Moor Road. This is the Limestone Way and leads all the way back to Monyash. For the remainder of the route there are Limestone Way symbols on nearly every post and stile to help find the way.

Keeping roughly in the same direction the Limestone Way passes through many fields, below a farm and through two wooded areas before it drops dramatically down through trees by way of some very slippery limestone steps to reach a valley bottom. This is Cales Dale.

At cross paths in the bottom take a narrow path straight across signposted for One Ash Grange Farm. Yet another tricky section through woods soon leads into a field, and then on to steps leading to the farm. Take time here to look at a shrine on the right in old outbuildings, and disused pig stys from the Georgian era. There is also an outbuilding on the farm where ice creams can usually be bought. Passing through the middle of the farm, the path bends right on to a green lane for a short while. As the lane bends sharp right take a path straight in front to stay in the same direction.

The rest of the route is fairly straight forward and basically involves staying on this path which becomes a green lane again as it comes into Monyash. Turn right and follow the road back into the village.

Look out for…..

Monyash is one of the few villages in Derbyshire which has a village green. Situated on the green is an old market cross the base of which dates back to the 14th century when Monyash was granted a charter to hold a weekly market. The holes in the stone are supposed to have been made by miners testing their drills after they had been sharpened in the village. Monyash was an important centre for lead mining in the 14th century.

Batemans House. Over the little wooden bridge across the river is Batemans House. The house was built over a very deep mine shaft sometime in the 1840's for Thomas Bateman who was agent of the Lathkill Mine, and lived there with his family. Within the ruined buildings is an access ladder to the shaft viewing level where there is a hand crank which generates electricity to power display lights.

Meadow Place Grange. Buildings have known to be on this site since 1066, although none that old currently remain there. Amongst the buildings still in use is the farmhouse which is a Grade II listed building and dates from the mid 18c. Like many properties in the area, Meadow Place Grange has strong religious connections, and a grange associated with Leicester Abbey is recorded at this site in 1251 and a chapel built in the early 1700s was demolished in 1851.

One Ash Grange Farm was once a farming outpost belonging to Roche Abbey near Rotherham and dates back to 1147. As a punishment, monks who had misbehaved at Roche Abbey were sent to One Ash Grange. Amongst the numerous farm buildings, the small building beside the path is thought to have been used by the monks as a cold store. The row of four pigstys are Grade II listed, and date back to 18c.

Dog Suitability

This is not a walk where dogs can be off-lead very much as there are sheep throughout Lathkill Dale, and both sheep and cows in a lot of the fields passed through on the way back. There are green lanes and wooded areas which are suitable for off-lead walking though.

Refreshments

In Monyash there is the Bulls Head pub, and the Old Smithy Tearooms, both situated next to the village green.

Walk No 6 : Wharncliffe Crags

8.5 miles / 4 hours

Introduction

This is a walk of two halves. Leaving from Grenoside, the first part is entirely on good woodland paths, shared with cyclists, passing through Wharncliffe Woods in the direction of Deepcar. The second part meanwhile is entirely different as a steady climb is taken through silver birch trees and heathland on to the top of Wharncliffe Crags, followed by a glorious 1.5 mile path along the top of the Crags. From here there are fantastic views up the Upper Don Valley, and of the Ewden Valley and beyond. It truly is a wonderful place to walk, especially as there never seems to be many people up there. Further on, after passing a couple of remote farms, the next part of the route crosses Wharncliffe Chase before finishing with a bit more woodland walking.

Autumn scene at the top of Wharncliffe Crags

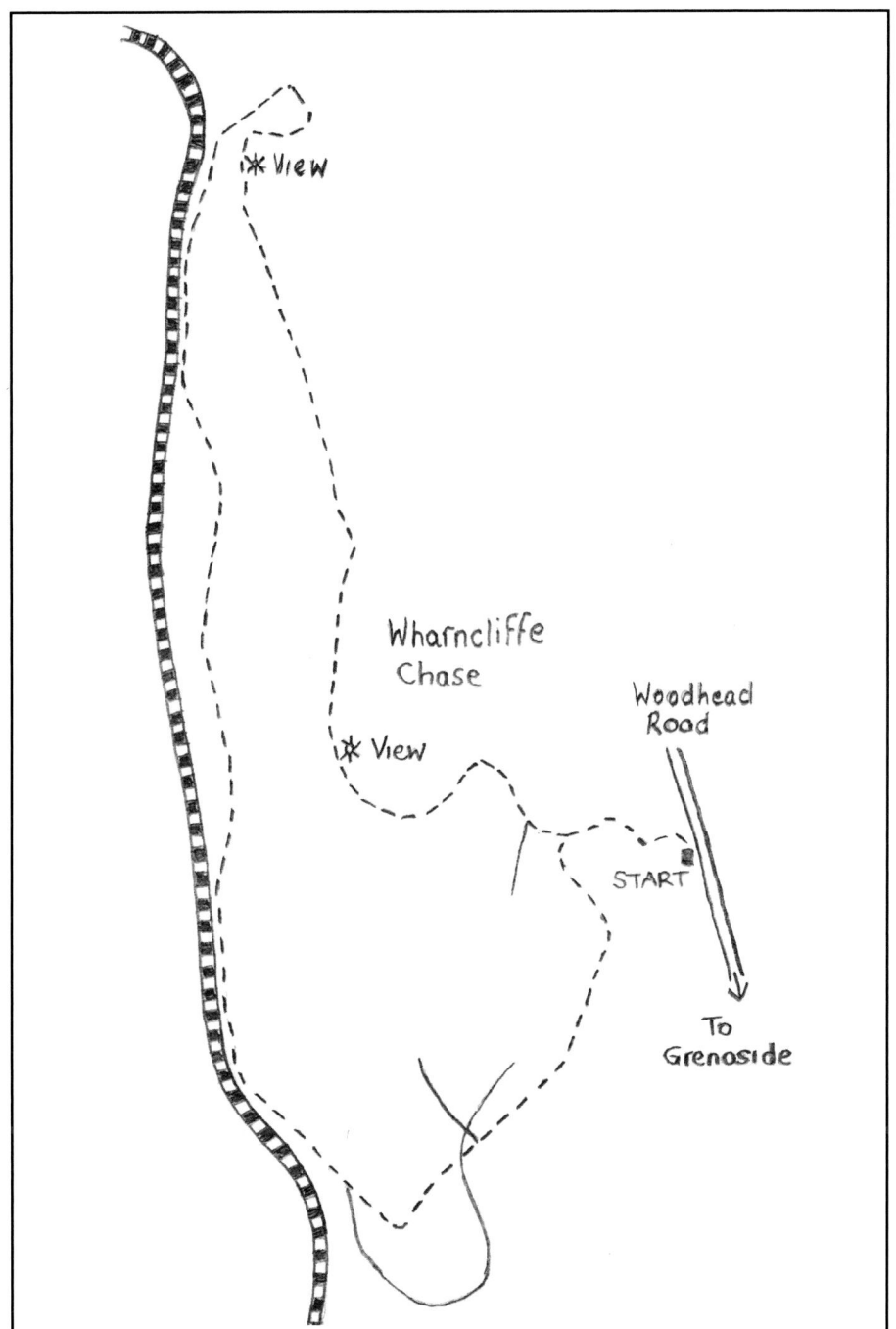

Walk Difficulty

There is not much in the way of steep hills on this walk as the climb up to the top of the Crags is steady, although the last half a mile back up through the woods can feel tough after 7.5 miles! The path along the top is quite rocky, so boots or strong shoes are definitely recommended for this walk.

Starting Point

Grenoside Wood Car Park, Woodhead Rd, Grenoside, Sheffield S35 8RS. What3Words: **jabs.deputy.strict**

The Route

From the car park take the wide track opposite the car park entrance which heads off steeply downhill. After half a mile at a track junction fork left. The track on the right is used later on in the walk to return to the car park. Stay on this track which carries on downhill for almost another mile until at a clearing, a number of other tracks can be seen going right and left. Ignore the first two tracks right, then at a fork, go right to stay in the same direction, still going downhill. Very soon, the track passes beneath power lines and sweeps right and is joined by another track coming up from the left.

The track stays lower down in the woods now for over three miles, all the way with a railway line not far away through the trees on the left. After three quarters of a mile though, there is a choice of routes at a fork, with both tracks meeting back up further on. Slightly shorter (and less hilly) is the left fork which has been chosen for this route. After half a mile the track is joined by the alternative route and carries on in the same direction. Very soon, the track starts to slowly climb, leaving the rail track down below, and after a further mile, an electricity pylon is reached on the right, with a gate next to it.

Through the gate is a rocky, direct route which climbs steeply to get on to the Crags. A better route though is to stay on the track for a further 250 yards to reach a path on the right, which although isn't signposted, is clearly a well-used path heading uphill. The bonus for taking this path too is that after a minute or two, at the top of some steps is a pond where to the left is an ideal spot to sit on the concreted edge of the pond for a refreshments break.

With the pond on the left, bear right to reach a gate. The path is climbing steadily now, and through the gate as the path bends left, there are great views of the Upper Don Valley, looking across to Deepcar. The path now stays at the top of the Crags for a mile and a half, still climbing to start with, but pretty soon levelling out as after half a mile it is joined by a wall on the left. The path stays close to the wall for three quarters of a mile, including at a fork where the left choice must be taken. Further on, the path leaves the wall by going slight right about 25 yards before a metal gate on the left.

With more outstanding views of the valley opening up, the path carries on for another quarter of a mile before it reaches a tarmacced farm road. In open land now, the road passes between farms and goes through a gate on to Wharncliffe Chase. Now a track, three quarters of a mile further on, after bending left, take a path on the right towards trees. At a wall go over a wall stile and turn left onto a track uphill. Keep left at the fork passed earlier on in the walk to return to the car park.

Look out for…..

Upper Don Valley. For a lot of the first half of the walk the path used runs above the River Don for about three miles, but it can't be seen for the trees in between. Just after the climb up on to the Crags, the Don Valley can be seen down below, as the river turns 45 degrees left to pass through Deepcar and Stocksbridge on its way to the distant Underbank Reservoir.

Ewden Valley. Just before the path along the top leaves the Crags, More Hall and Broomhead reservoirs can be seen in the Ewden Valley across the Don Valley. These two reservoirs form part of the 14 reservoirs which make up Sheffield Lakeland, along with Underbank Reservoir seen earlier.

Dog Suitability

Dogs can be off-lead all walk, apart from at the start of the climb on to the Crags, where there might be cows, and ground-nesting birds in springtime.

Refreshments

There are four pubs and a shop, just down the road in Grenoside village.

FOOTHILLS

THE WALKING SPECIALISTS SINCE 1993

11 EDGEDALE ROAD
SHEFFIELD
S7 2BQ

ROHAN & PARAMO PREMIER STOCKISTS

EXPERT BOOT FITTING BY APPOINTMENT ACROSS AN EXTENSIVE RANGE INCLUDING MEINDL, ALTBERG & ZAMBERLAN

10% OFF FOR MEMBERS OF RAMBLING GROUPS

OVER 25 YEARS OF KNOWLEDGE & EXPERTISE

0114 2586228
SALES@FOOTHILLS.COM

WWW.FOOTHILLS.UK.COM

Walk No 7 : Grindleford

5.25 miles / 2.5 hours

Introduction

This is quite a challenging walk but all the more rewarding for it, as it includes many different types of scenery along the way. Starting with a field path alongside the River Derwent, the route then takes an old packhorse track, Spooner Lane to reach the picturesque village of Froggatt. From there, it's a stiff climb up to Froggatt Edge to enjoy outstanding views of the Hope Valley. The top of this edge is a lovely place to sit and have a picnic on a sunny day, although it can get quite busy with other walkers in summer. After walking a decent stretch along Froggatt Edge, the return to the start is made via a long downhill section through Hay Wood to reach Upper Padley. Then after passing through the village, it's field paths all the way back to Grindleford.

Looking down to Grindleford from Froggatt Edge

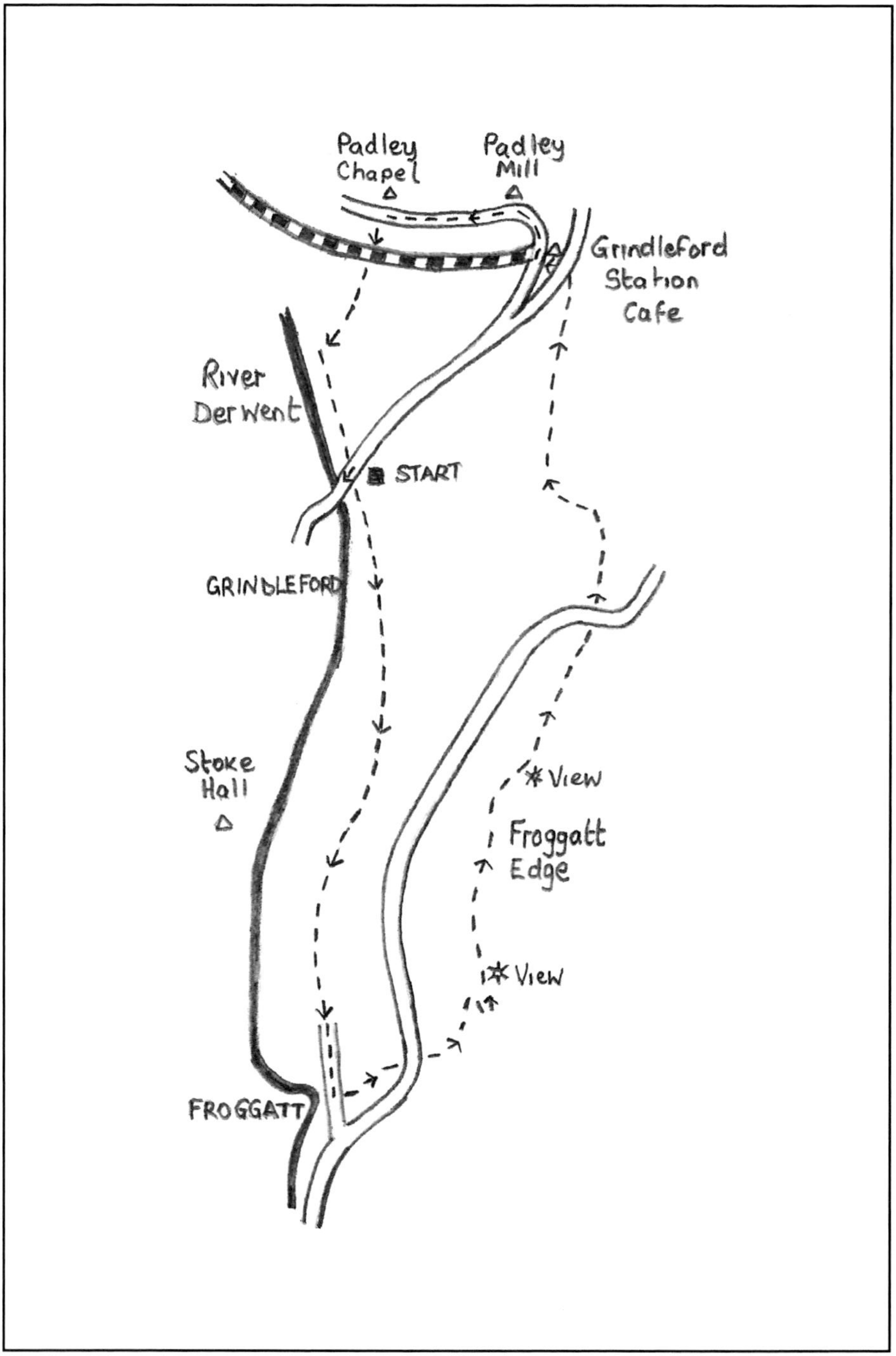
Padley Chapel
Padley Mill
Grindleford Station Cafe
River Derwent
START
GRINDLEFORD
Stoke Hall
View
Froggatt Edge
View
FROGGATT

Walk Difficulty

As well as the steep uphill section up to the Edge, there are some tricky downhill sections along rocky paths on the way back.

Starting Point

The main road (B6521) outside St Helens Church, Grindleford, S32 2JN. What3Words: **crumb.link.slam.** The walk could also start at Grindleford station where car parking charges apply.

The Route

Walk along the road towards the village, and after a few yards take a path on the left which enters a field. Cross the field diagonally to the far-left corner, keeping to the left of a large tree to cross a stream. The path now leads uphill with trees and bushes on the right to reach a gate. Going through the gate the path becomes cobbled and carries on for quite a while through woods until it enters a field, carrying on in the same direction. After going through a 2nd field at the 3rd field the path goes diagonally right towards a wall. At the corner of the wall the path carries on with the wall on its left to reach a gate.

Go through a stile next to the gate to go on to a narrow track between walls which after a short while becomes a road alongside houses. At the junction keep in the same direction, soon passing a bridge over the river on the right. About 100 yards after the bridge take a path on the left just before the road bends. The path climbs uphill through scrubland to reach the main road. Cross the road on to a path into woods. Ignore an immediate path left and keep right as this path climbs up, often steeply to reach a rockface. At this point turn right to carry on rising with the rockface on your left. At the top, turn left on to a wide track along Froggatt Edge.

Stay on this track along the Edge until after a mile it reaches a fork. Stay left and the path soon drops down and bends right to reach the main road again. Turn right to walk along the road for 40 yards before crossing the road to go through a gate opposite. The path leads down a banking to a stream which must be crossed to then go up the banking at the other side.

Into trees the path passes to the left of a car park. About 30 yards past the car park take the feint path to the left which leads on to a downhill path through a gully. Further down at cross paths carry on going downhill, then at the second cross paths take a path right. Very soon the path reaches a gate leading on to a road. Walk along this road which after just under half a mile reaches the main road. Cross the road and walk round the bend to find a path on the left which drops steeply down to Grindleford station. Turn right on to the road which passes the café, and after going over a railway bridge bends left to pass through Upper Padley.

After passing the chapel on the right, the track reaches a cattle grid. Once over the grid take a path on the left which crosses over the railway. After a minute or two on this path take a signposted path left into a field. At the far side of the field the path reaches a wall. From there the path stays close to the wall and leads through marshland and into trees at the bottom. At a path going left and right go left and after immediately crossing a stream there are two path options in the next field. By going half right there is a lovely path next to the river. Alternatively a more direct route is to go straight forward through this long field, but either way they both meet up in the far corner of the field at a gate which is opposite the church.

Look out for…….

Grindleford which is thought to have either been named after "the ford where grindstones crossed the river, or because the original ford had become too deep for use and had been "ground away".

Stoke Hall is a stately hall in miniature, built in 1757 in local stone from nearby Stoke Hall Quarry. Before this there were a number of other residences called Stoke Hall dating back to the Domesday Book. Famous owners of Stoke Hall include the Barlows of Barlow Hall in 15c, Bess of Hardwick in 16c, the Cavendish family in the 17c, and cutlery manufacturer Emile Viner in 1950's. Bess of Hardwick was famous for how she rose through English society through a series of marriages. Three of her husbands were Barlow, Cavendish and Talbot, the Earl of Shrewsbury. While Bess was married to Talbot she worked on needlework embroideries with Mary Queen of Scots whilst she was imprisoned at Chatsworth House.

Fair Flora is a statue which stands in woodlands within the grounds of Stoke Hall. In the 19th century Flora was a servant at the Hall and was allegedly brutally killed there. Her employers erected a statue to her memory which for a while was reputed to move positions in the woods whilst her ghost is said to haunt the hall.

Padley Mill was built in 18c and served as a corn mill, sawmill and wire-drawing mill until becoming derelict in the early 1900's. It was subsequently renovated and in the 1930's became a café for a short while, serving walkers. It is now a Grade ll listed building and has been converted into a residence.

Dog Suitability

This is not a great walk for dogs to be off lead, due to the possibility of there being sheep in the fields near Grindleford, and on parts of Froggatt Edge. On the climb up to the edge, and the descent through Hay Wood dogs can run free.

Refreshments

There is a community café at Grindleford church which has limited opening hours, then there is the very popular Grindleford Station café for a choice of places to enjoy refreshments.

Walk No 8 : Parkwood Springs

4.25 miles / 2.5 hours

Introduction

This walk is all about the views, and Sheffield's inner city Country Park. Situated high above the Don Valley, and only just over a mile from the city centre, Parkwood Springs is an amazing place to visit, and this walk covers much of what the park has to offer. After a look round the heath and wood land at the top of Parkwood the route leads on to one of the views from the skyline path; a viewpoint looking over the Rutland Road area, with Sheffield city centre and Peak District hills in the distance. From there, it's a downhill section through an old quarry, and the site of the old ski village to reach an industrial area next to the River Don. Following a stroll along the river, and a visit to Wardsend Cemetery, the route heads back up to the top of Parkwood and more great views from the WW2 gun emplacements, on the way back through more woodland to return to the start.

Sheffield City Centre from the skyline path

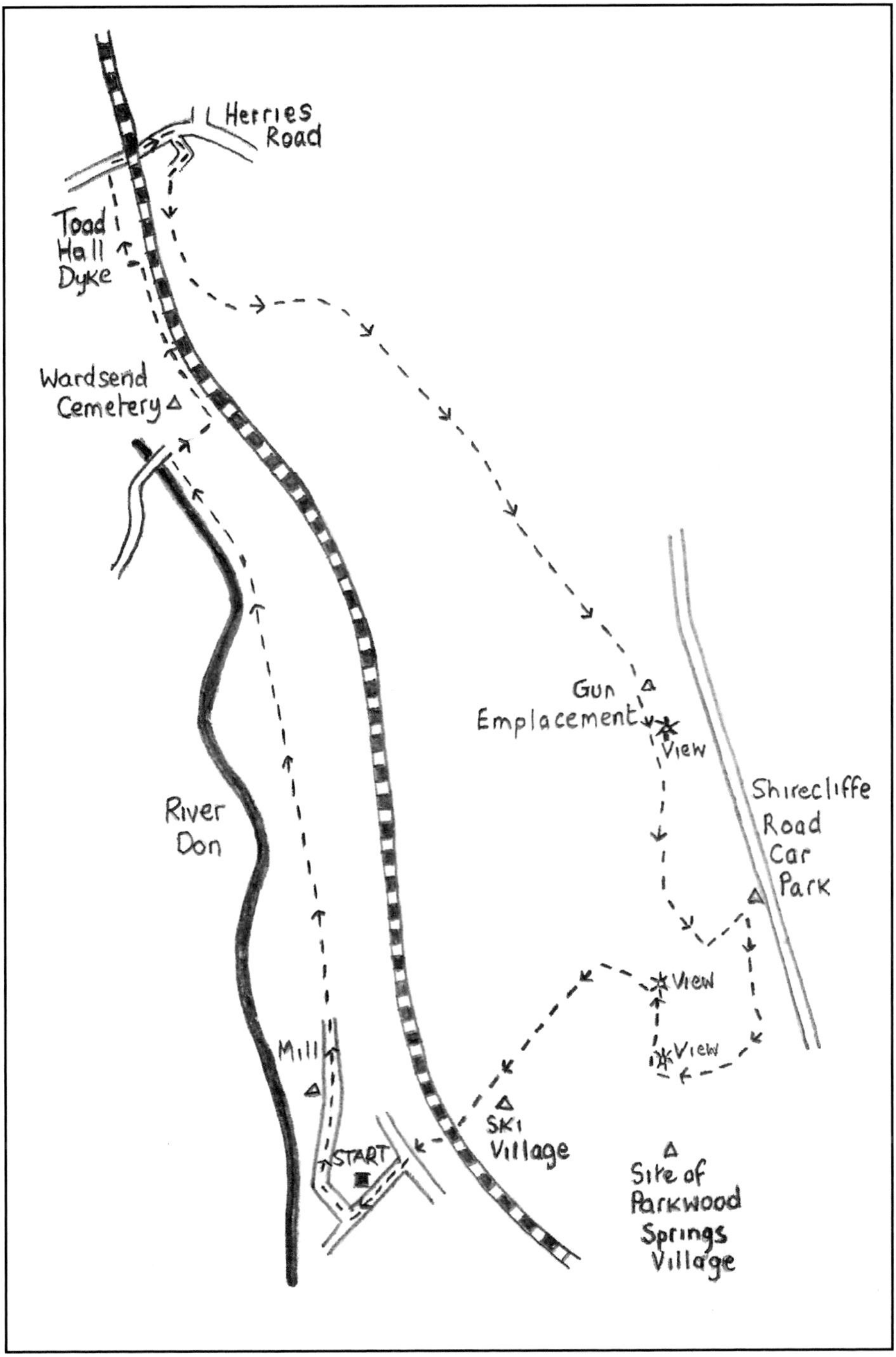
Herries Road
Toad Hall Dyke
Wardsend Cemetery
River Don
Gun Emplacement
View
Shirecliffe Road Car Park
View
View
Mill
START
Ski Village
Site of Parkwood Springs Village

Walk Difficulty

The walk takes place on mainly good paths, but there is some rough ground, and parts of the walk can be muddy and slippy after rain and in winter. Although the climb to the top is fairly steady, the path down through the quarry can be a bit of a challenge.

Starting Point

The starting point is Sandbed Road at Neepsend. A nearby postcode is S3 8AB What3Words for Sandbed Road: **brave.toxic.focus.** The walk can also be started at Parkwood Springs car park, Shirecliffe Lane, S3 9AA. What3Words: **curl.daily.asks.** Check in advance for the car park opening times though.

The Route

At the bottom of Sandbed Road turn right on to Club Mill Lane. Stay on this road to pass through industrial units, and carry on in the same direction as the road becomes an unsurfaced track. After about a mile the track reaches a bridge over the river on the left. Take the steps opposite leading up into Wardsend Cemetery. At the top of the steps take a look at the site of the old cemetery chapel on the right, and then return to the main path. Carry on uphill and as the path reaches a bridge across the railway turn left and take this narrow path with a metal fence and railway line on the right. Stay on this path next to the railway, and very soon a path can be seen down below to the left which the route goes on to a little further on. To start with, ignore the many steep minor paths which have been made on the left to reach this path, until after about 300 yards the path reaches a clearing.

Go down the banking here to reach the lower path, then turn right. The path goes steeply downhill for a minute or two, then almost at the bottom of the hill a bridge across the quaintly named Toad Hall Dyke can be seen on the left. Carry on for about 30 yards past the bridge, then take a path on the left which doubles back to cross the bridge. Over the bridge the path turns right and soon leads to steps leading on to Herries Road. Turn right to walk up the hill for just under a quarter a mile, then turn right on to Scraith Wood Drive and stay on this road as it bends to the right and climbs steadily.

At the top of the road take a path between houses in the left corner. The path keeps in same direction through scrubland, soon to be joined by a path coming down from the left, keeping in the same direction. When the path meets a track on a bend, go straight across onto the track, with corrugated fencing on the right and smallholdings behind it. Further on as the track bends sharp left go straight-forward on to a path with a hedge on the right to pass more smallholdings. The path enters trees and stays at roughly the same level, until after about 200 yards it bends left to head towards houses. Just before the houses the path reaches a junction of paths at the top of the hill. Cross over the main path in front to go through trees half right on to a large open area. Here, take the path left and then after about 40 yards fork left again. Reaching a track going left and right there are two paths ahead heading up a banking. Take the right one, although the paths meet back up again in a couple of minutes higher up the banking.

After the path emerges into open scrubland it begins to level out and the other path joins it from the left. At this point old local-authority built houses can be seen to the left. About 50 yards further on take the right fork in the direction of newer houses in the distance. Reaching the far left corner of the scrubland the path goes through a motor bike prevention gate and on to an enclosed path with a hedge to the left and a fence with the old landfill site behind it on the right. After about 150 yards the path bends left to go up a small banking. At the top, ignore the path straight ahead into a housing estate to take the steps right to stay on the path between houses and the old landfill site. After passing through another gate the path reaches the corner of a football pitch. Keep in the same direction here, on to an obvious path which keeps to the right of the football pitch.

After passing the site of the WW2 anti-aircraft guns on the left, the path reaches an observation post on the right. Take a little time here to take in the views across to Hillsborough, Walkley and the Upper Don Valley. Back on the path, keep in the same direction, then after a few yards bear left on to a path which goes downhill through trees. At cross paths go straight forward to come out of the trees and on to grass leading to a wide path below. Cross the path onto playing fields, then go half left across the fields towards a metal gate on the edge of woodland.

Through the gate the path leads downhill with houses to the left. Stay close to the houses, carrying on downhill until a pond is reached on the right. The path leads round the pond and levels out. Ignore any paths or cycle tracks leading away from this path until after just over 200 yards the main path joins up from the left. Keep in the same direction on this path which soon bends to the right and offers great views across the city. As the path starts to climb it passes a bench next to another great viewing point. Just past the bench the path bends to the right to head into trees. After 40 yards leave the main path to fork left, passing the remains of the old ski slopes on the left. Where this path reaches another path coming up from the right there are two paths left.

The first one just leads to the top of the ski slope; it is the one next to it which is needed to leave the hillside and head to the valley below through an old quarry. To start with the path descends gently between bankings. Soon though, the descent becomes steeper and the path bends to the left at a metal fence for the landfill site. Stay close to the fence, carrying on downhill until after just under half a mile after leaving the top, the path reaches enclosed steps leading down to a railway bridge. Cross the bridge, then go down more steps to reach Parkwood Road. Go right, then take the next road left to walk back down to Sandbed Road.

Look out for…..

Parkwood Springs Village was mainly situated on the lower part of the hillside between Rutland Road and the ski village. It had a population of 3000 and 25% of the houses were bombed during WW2. The whole area fell into dereliction, and the houses were demolished in the 1970's.

Old Park Silver Mill at Neepsend was established in the 1760's by a Mr. Joseph Hancock, the first person to use water power to roll Sheffield Plate, a fusion of Copper and Silver. Prior to this, as a corn mill, it was called Club Mill, due to its joint 'club' ownership of four owners, which eventually gave Club Mill Lane its name. At the time the Corn Mill provided the owners with cost price-flour. As a silver mill it produced items such as candlesticks, snuff boxes, tea pots and coffee pots. In 1864, when the Dale Dike dam burst, the resulting flood completely destroyed one mill shop and its furnaces . The insurance claim for totalled £1,932, which was a huge amount in those days.

Wardsend Cemetery began being used in 1857 and had its last burial in 1968. It is the only cemetery in the country which has an active railway line going through it. The graveyard holds many victims of the Great Sheffield Flood of 1864, and due to its close locality to Hillsborough Barracks, it also has a great number of service personnel from the 2 World Wars.

1862 cemetery riot. On the evening of 3rd June 1862, the cemetery was the location of a turbulent riot by angry Sheffield citizens, who accused the local vicar and his sexton of neglecting to bury corpses, and instead selling them to the town's medical school for use in anatomical dissection. The rumours were proven false, however the 2 of them were later fined for reusing graves in order to save space.

Toad Hall Dyke. Originally 'T'owd Hall Dyke' in local speak. The stream flows down from Southey where there was an old hall which was demolished in 1937. In other words, a dyke from the Hall!

Gun Emplacement. On the skyline path, behind the top football pitch, is a stone pad, a remnant of a Second World War anti-aircraft gun emplacement. As nearby areas had suffered casualties in a Zeppelin raid in the First World War, the hilltop was soon put into use in WW2 as an Anti-Aircraft post, and by December 1940 there were heavy Anti-Aircraft guns positioned on top of the hill. A rocket based emplacement called a Z battery was also manned there by the Home Guard, but rumour has it that more damage was caused by the rockets falling short on to the city down below, than was caused by the Luftwaffe.

Dog Suitability

Dogs can be off-lead for almost all of the walk. There are just two short road walking sections when they will need to be led.

Refreshments

A kiosk/café is planned for the car park at Parkwood at the time of writing, otherwise there is a variety of pubs and cafes to get food and drink from at Kelham Island, or shops just over the hill at Norwood.

Walk No 9 : The Great Ridge

9 miles / 5 hours

Introduction

The Great Ridge is one of the great walks of the Peak District, and the views on both sides of the ridge are well worth the effort needed to get up there in the first place. Leaving from the village of Hope, the route starts with a gentle section alongside Peakshole Water to reach Castleton, before it heads off up Cave Dale and the climb which eventually leads to the top of Mam Tor. Along Back Tor, the route then reaches Lose Hill before dropping down through fields to return to Hope. Cameras or phone cameras are a must for this walk.

Lose Hill viewed from close to Peakshole Water

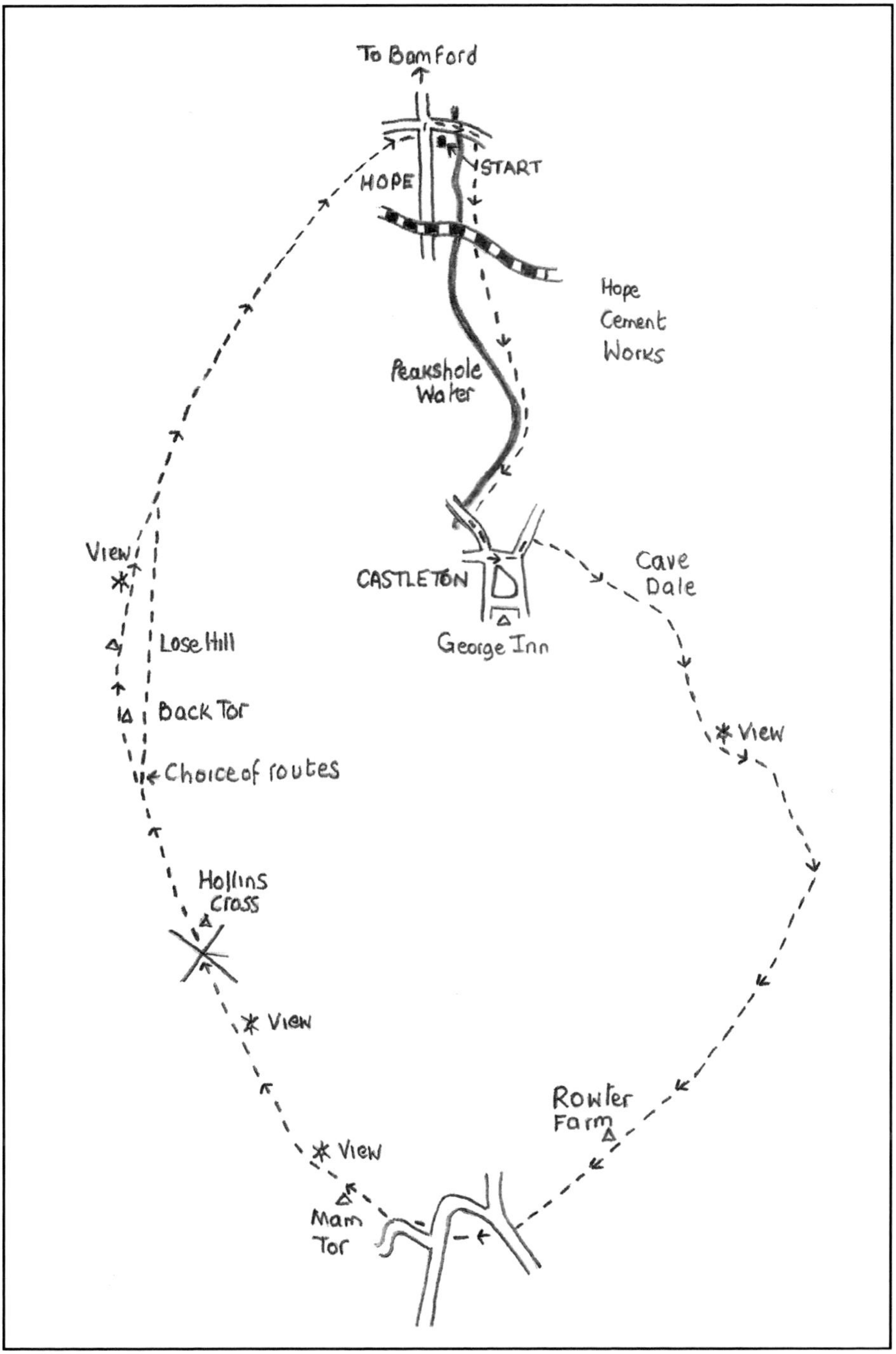
To Bamford
HOPE
START
Hope
Cement
Works
Peakshole
Water
CASTLETON
George Inn
Cave
Dale
View
View
Lose Hill
Back Tor
Choice of routes
Hollins
Cross
View
Rowter
Farm
View
Mam
Tor

Walk Difficulty

The climb up Cave Dale is a difficult one, although very rewarding at the same time. Care needs to be taken underfoot here due to the loose stones and rocks on the path, especially in winter when there can be the additional challenges of water running down the hill, plus ice which can also make the ascent extremely tricky. Further on, there is also the upper section of Mam Tor to scale, whilst along the Great Ridge, the route up Back Tor if chosen is also a bit of a challenge. On the way down from the Ridge, some of the field paths can be slippery too.

Starting Point

The public car park in the centre of Hope has been chosen as the starting point for this walk, but Castleton could equally be used to begin from. The address for the car park is Castleton Road, Hope, S33 6RS. What3Words: **hotel.feasting.perfume**

The Route

Coming out of the car park turn right to walk along the road. Pass the Woodroffe Arms then turn right to walk down Pindale Road. After crossing a bridge, the road starts to climb. After about 50 yards, take a signed path on the right which skirts round a field, with trees and a drop down to the river on the right. Stay on this path close to the river for a while, but then after crossing a railway line it leaves the river to keep in the same direction, passing the Hope Valley Cement Works as it heads towards Castleton. Re-joining the river further on, the path eventually reaches the main road.

Turn left to walk into Castleton, staying on the road as it bends left. At a second bend, go straight ahead, keeping to the left of the Nags Head. Stay to the left of the village green, then after 30 yards take a signposted path on the right between houses to enter Cave Dale. Stay on this rocky path as it climbs very steeply to start with through the limestone gorge. Staying in roughly the same direction the path eventually levels out, and after one and a quarter miles reaches two large gates in quick succession. Through the second gate there is a track going left and right. Go right to go through another gate, then after about 200 yards fork right to head towards Rowter Farm in the distance.

Passing to the left of the farm, in just under a mile the track reaches a road. Cross to a path opposite and carry on in the same direction to reach another road. With Mam Tor looming up ahead on the right, cross the road on to a path which climbs up to Mam Nick and the road to Edale. At the road, turn right onto a signposted path which leads sharply uphill on a stepped path which leads to the summit of Mam Tor. At the top, pass to the right of the trig point to stay on the top of the ridge for almost one and a half miles. About half way along this section, the path passes Hollins Cross which is a famous cross roads of paths which has an obelisk in the middle of it. About half a mile after this, with a gate to the left, there is a choice of routes.

For a difficult challenge, by going through the gate and then turning right, there is the opportunity to climb Back Tor to enjoy the outstanding views from up there. If this option is taken, once the summit of Back Tor has been reached, the path carries on in the same direction to reach the top of Lose Hill. From here the path bends right to leave the hill. After going down a steep section the path reaches a stile. Over the stile, fork right to reach another stile. Over this stile turn left to carry on going downhill.

Meanwhile, for the second option just carry straight on at the gate to enter pine trees, and stay on this path as it leaves the wood to stay at roughly the same level, and to start with in the same direction. After about half a mile the path starts to bend right, and also descend as it is joined by the other path coming down from the left. The path now descends quickly to reach a farm, passing to the left of it. Over a stile, take a path on the right which leads through a succession of fields and stiles as it carries on downhill.

Further down, as a minor path joins it from the right, the path bends slightly to the left to become enclosed as it heads towards a small settlement. Go straight forward here to pass through buildings, keeping straight on to reach a path and bridge over a railway. At the other side the path carries on through small fields and an enclosed path until it reaches a housing estate. Cross the road on to a road opposite, then just as the road bends right, take a signposted path left which goes between houses to reach Castleton Road. Turn right to quickly return to the starting point.

Look out for…..

Peakshole Water which is 2.75 miles long and flows from under Peak Cavern down to the River Noe at Hope.

The Hope Valley Cement Works Railway Line is 2 miles long and carries almost all of the 1.3 million tons of cement produced at the works every year.

Cave Dale was initially formed by melting glaciers carving a deep narrow valley in the limestone. The river then found a route underground leaving a dry valley with caverns underneath. Later on, the caverns below Cave Dale collapsed making the valley even deeper and gorge-like. The Castleton entrance to Cave Dale had a narrow natural arch as recently as 200 years ago before it collapsed. The loose stones have been caused by frost causing the rocks higher up in the cliffs to shatter.

Lose Hill and its sister Win Hill, according to folklore, were named after a 7c battle between the Kings of Northumbria and Wessex. There is no evidence that this ever happened though, just word of mouth stories!

Mam Tor Hill Fort was situated on top of the hill, with ramparts being in evidence further down the hill indicating that it was a large Iron Age fort. However, a Bronze Age axe head found close to where the Trig point is, suggests that Mam Tor was inhabited in the Bronze Age. Mam Tor meaning Mother Hill.

Dog Suitability

There are likely to be sheep on most parts of this walk, so dogs would have to be kept under close control throughout.

Refreshments

There is a good choice of pubs, cafes and shops in both Hope and Castleton including the excellent George Inn at Castleton.

Walk No 10 : Wortley

7.5 miles / 4 hours

Introduction

Just a mile or two outside Sheffield is Wortley, a picturesque village surrounded by rolling countryside. Being where it is, it means that this walk is neither in Sheffield nor the Peak District, but it is such a good walk, it is definitely worth a place in the book. With history all around it, this is a good all-round walk to enjoy, and although it takes place mainly on field paths and farm tracks, there is also a small amount of road walking. The history begins at the starting point with Wortley Church, which has a link to a 5c French monk. The history then carries on with the site of a tin mill and a well-preserved old forge on the banks of the River Don, both of which came to prominence during the 18c Industrial Revolution. Following a trek through the fields surrounding Wortley, the route carries on through the Wharncliffe Estate to Wortley Hall, originally the ancestral home of the Earls of Wharncliffe, the Lords of the Manor of Wortley.

St Leonards church in Wortley

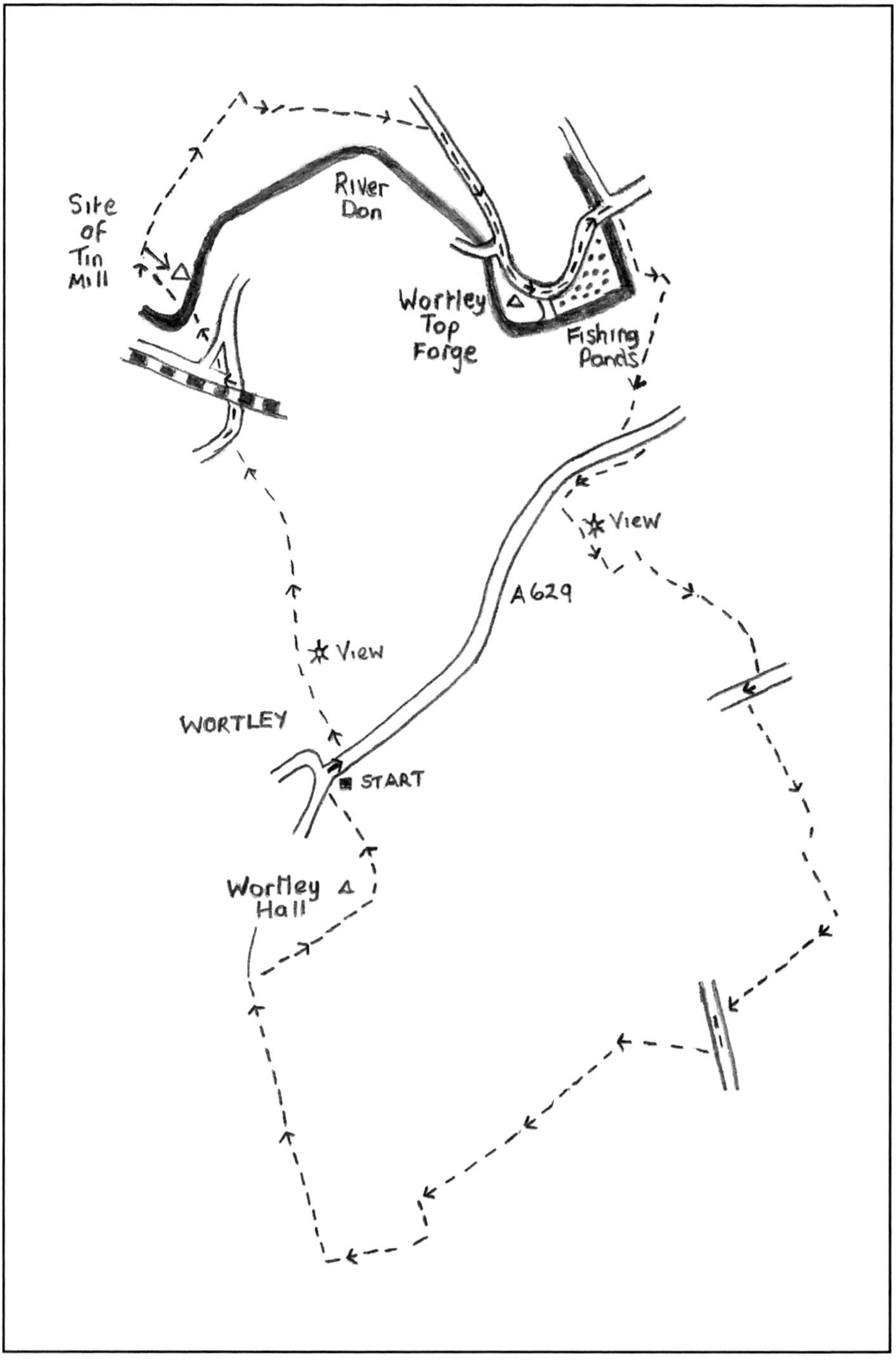
Site of Tin Mill
River Don
Wortley Top Forge
Fishing Ponds
View
A629
View
WORTLEY
START
Wortley Hall

Walk Difficulty

There are no great ascents or descents on this walk, but there are quite a lot of stiles to tackle, and some of the paths can get very muddy in winter.

Starting Point

Outside the Countess Tearooms, Park Avenue, Wortley, S35 7DB.
What3Words: **ponies.shelving.loaf**

The Route

From the Countess Tearooms, cross the main road on the bend and turn right. Where the churchyard ends take a signposted path left which leads into a field. Stay on this path as it drops downhill, and after half a mile comes out on to a main road. Cross the road to walk right, then after passing under a bridge take the road left. After a few yards cross the road to take a path in the middle of bushes. This path crosses a field to come out on to a side road with cottages left. Cross this road on to another path which leads down to the River Don. Either cross it by the bridge, or by the stepping stones.

Over the other side, take a track opposite, Tin Mill Lane, then after a few yards take another track right which leads uphill through woods. The track ends after a quarter of a mile at a stile and becomes a path which gets a bit tricky the further up it goes. Eventually at a stile, the path enters a field. Turn right here and walk along the bottom of the field with a wall and woods to the right. Further on, take a stile on the right to go back into the woods and stay on this path which stays high up in the woods next to a steep drop.

After a few minutes the path reaches cottages and passes through the middle of them to reach a road. Walk down the road for a quarter of a mile, turning left on to Forge Lane to pass the entranceway to Wortley Top Forge. The road passes fishing ponds on the right, then just after passing a white house on the left the road crosses a bridge over the River Don. On the other side take an immediate path down steps on the right. Stay on this path next to the River Don for about 100 yards, then at a fork leave the river to reach a path 'T' junction. Turn left to climb up what was an old railway embankment.

Before the path reaches the top of the banking go through a tunnel on the right and stay on this path as it bends right and stays next to a wire fence for about 50 yards. The path ends at a stile on the left which leads into a sheep field. In the distance can be seen the A629 which needs to be crossed once the path reaches it. The route from here though goes half right, and leads up and across a large field marked by five marker posts. The first two come quickly together with the second one being reached just before a ditch. After crossing the ditch go half left towards a silver birch tree. Cross another ditch just above this tree, then the next three markers to follow can be seen up ahead. Almost at the top of the field, over the wall to the left, a footpath sign can be seen on the other side of the road. This sign indicates the next path to take once the road is crossed.

After going over the stile to reach the A629, cross the road and turn left to walk along the road for about 40 yards. At the signpost just mentioned take the path right, then after a few yards take a path to the right which cuts through trees alongside the main road. After about 5 minutes the path reaches a track going left and right. Turn left here on to this enclosed track between fields. After just over a quarter of a mile the track reaches a farm. Turn left here on to a grass path to pass a house, and when the garden path ends take a path right. Through a gate carry on in the same direction keeping to the right of hawthorn bushes. In the left corner of the field cross an old stile on to a feint path through scrubland.

At the bottom of the field go left into a hedge, then after crossing a stile the path returns to the field to carry on in the same direction at the edge of the field with trees to the left. After 250 yards go through a gap in the bushes on the left and turn left to walk round the outside of the field heading for the far left corner. Once there, ignore the steep path straight ahead to go left instead, on to a path which bends right to re-join the first path at the bottom. After crossing a bridge look for steps to the left to climb up to a road. Turn right to walk up the road for about 100 yards then go over a stile on the left next to a gate. Go straight forward in the field staying to the left of a broken wall to start with, and then the odd tree further along. At the last hawthorn bush take a stile opposite on the left and then go right, staying close to the wall to start with. When the path leaves the wall it heads towards a fence in the distance where it crosses a bridge to go into a field.

There is no clear path next, however a sheep track going straight across can be taken towards an oak tree. Pass to the left of the tree, and as there is still no clear path, go half left across the field towards 2 more oak trees and in the direction of a high banking at the top of the field. Pass between the two trees and head for a footpath sign which will now be visible at the top of the banking. Go over the stile there, then go straight forwards, aiming for the last hawthorn bush on the right.

Pass to the right of the end bush and stay at the left side of the field, with a wire fence and bushes on the left. At the top left corner of the field go through a gate on to a path which leads to a road. Turn left here and walk along the road for a short way to take a path on the right opposite a farm. Again there is no clear path, but the route stays close to the hedge on the left to reach a stile on the left, at the bottom of the field. Over the stile the path carries on in the same direction in the next field, this time with the hedge now on the right. At the bottom of this field the path crosses a stile to enter woods and becomes quite narrow as it drops down to a track crossroads. Cross to a track opposite which after crossing a bridge over a stream heads uphill through more woods to emerge into a field at a gate.

Through the gate go straight forward on to a path between fields, then after 200 yards go left at the next field on to a path which goes round the outside of the field, bending right before it reaches a main track through the Wharncliffe Estate. Turn right on to the track and stay on it for nearly a mile until a path can be seen on the right leading to Wortley Hall. Turn right on to a path which passes the Hall and leads to a drive which bends left to pass cottages as it leaves the estate and returns to the start.

Look out for.....

St Leonards Church. Historically there is evidence that there has been a church in Wortley dedicated to St Leonard since at least 1268, and probably even earlier. The church there today dates from the 18th century, and there is little left of previous buildings on the site. Furthermore, there is no evidence whatsoever as to how a Yorkshire church became named after a 5th century French monk!

Wortley Tin Mill opened in 1743 and used water power from the River Don to roll wrought iron into thin sheets which were then coated with tin. The mill was owned by the Earl of Wharncliffe, and correspondence from 1887 relates to how the Earl of Wharncliffe was looking to sell off the machinery at the tin mill, as it had been 'blown up' in December of that year destroying the rolls. Historic map evidence shows that the site was in decline by the end of the 19th century and became derelict by the beginning of the 20th century.

Wortley Top Forge is the oldest surviving water powered iron forge in the world. The forge's history can be traced back to at least 1640 and during its working life the forge was most famous for producing wrought iron railway axles that were hammer-welded between 1840 and the closing of the Forge around 1910. Run by volunteers as a working industrial museum, the forge is normally open Sundays and Bank Holidays between Easter and November.

Wortley Hall was originally the ancestral home of the Earls of Wharncliffe, the Lords of the Manor of Wortley and has a number of historical connections. One is that during the Civil War, Sir Francis Wortley led the battle of Tankersley Moor from there, and was captured by Roundheads and taken to the Tower of London. During the second world war the Hall was requisitioned by the RAF as a munitions dump, before it was acquired by trade union and labour movements in 1950 for training and holiday purposes.

Wortley. The village is famous for the notorious highwayman Swift Nick, born in 1639. It was really he (not Dick Turpin) who made the infamous ride on horseback from London to York in order to establish an alibi for a robbery.

Dog Suitability

There are a few fields where dogs need to be led, and a small amount of road walking and crossing of roads, otherwise it's quite a good walk for dogs.

Refreshments

Halfway through the walk the route passes very close to the Bridge Inn at Thurgoland, and in Wortley, as well as the Countess tearooms, there is a shop next door and the Wortley Arms and Wortley Hall close by to obtain both food and drink.

Walk No 11 : Calver

5 miles / 3 hours

Introduction

Although this walk starts in Calver, it soon moves on to three other lovely villages, Stoney Middleton, Eyam and Froggatt through field tracks, old packhorse routes and some road walking. Each of these villages has it's own history, and there are many old buildings to check out along the way which have stories to tell. Stoney Middleton has it's unique church, Eyam has the plague history, and Froggatt has Aunt Flora reputedly haunting nearby Stoke Hall. There are also some excellent views from high up on the way to and from Eyam, and some lovely tea shops and touristy stuff in Eyam for anyone who has the time to stop off there.

The River Derwent near Calver

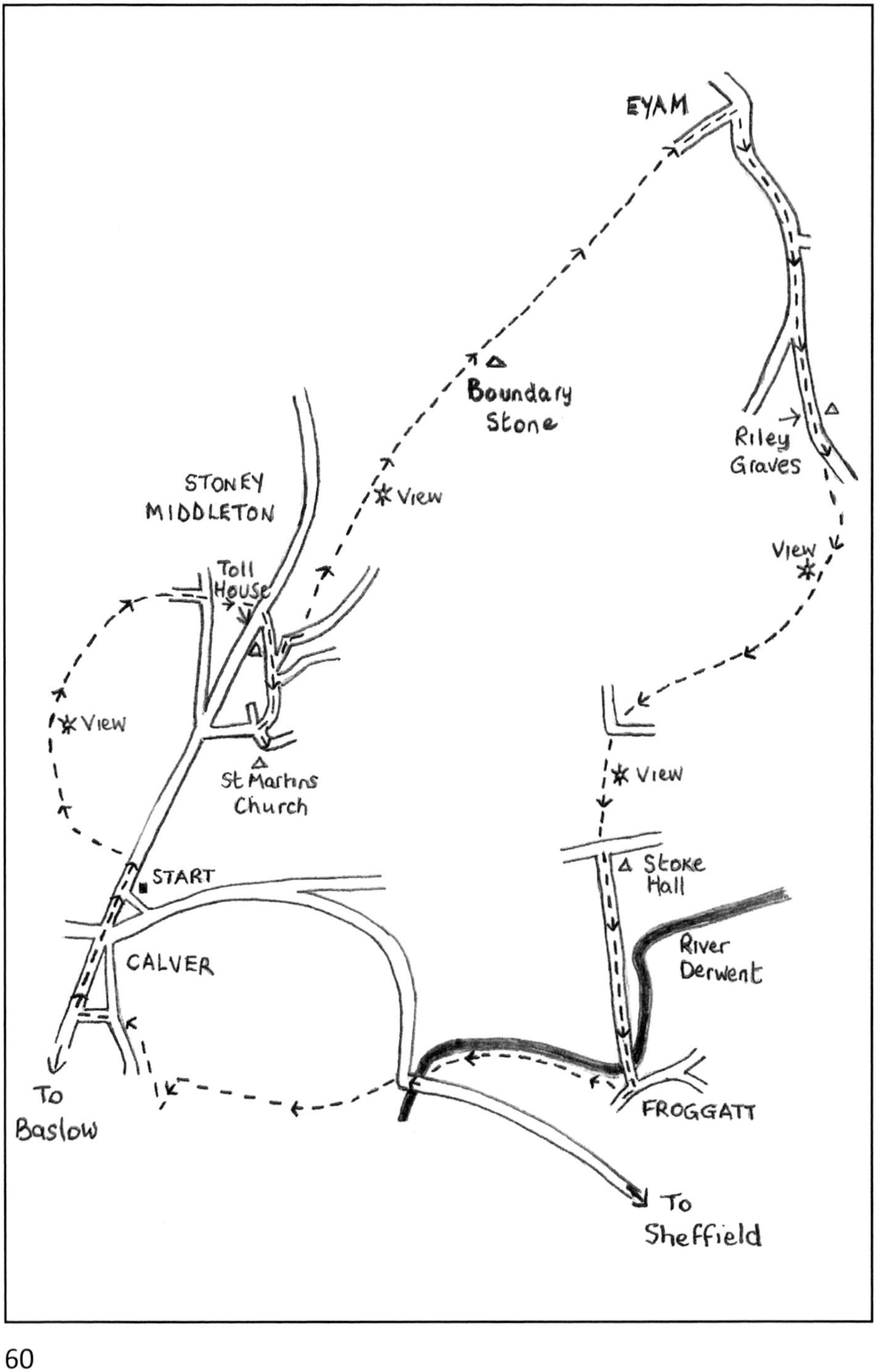
EYAM
Boundary Stone
Riley Graves
STONEY MIDDLETON
View
View
Toll House
View
View
St Martins Church
START
Stoke Hall
CALVER
River Derwent
To Baslow
FROGGATT
To Sheffield

Walk Difficulty

There are a few hills to climb, although none of them are too steep, and a couple of slightly tricky downhill sections to tackle along with some paths which can get muddy in winter. There is also a small amount of road walking.

Starting Point

Polly Froggatt Lane, opposite the Eyre Arms in Calver, S32 3XH. There is a small amount of parking there, otherwise it's parking along Sough Lane nearby. What3words is **lyricism.fall.tweed.**

The Route

From Polly Froggatt Lane walk along the main road in the direction of Stoney Middleton. At the sports ground cross the road to take a signposted track up the side of the football pitch. This is the start of Coombs Dale. After 250 yards take a signposted path right. The path soon goes half left, climbing a banking to reach a gate in a wall. The path carries on in the same direction, still climbing, to reach another gate at the top. From here the path heads towards a barn, passing to the right of it to reach a further gate to pass through.

Still keeping in roughly the same direction the path passes through a final gate next to a house, and then becomes a track and further on a tarmacced lane. This is Eaton Fold. At the end of the lane turn right to go downhill, then after a few yards take a steep path on the left, just before the school. At the bottom, cross the main road then take a road to the right which passes behind the chippy. To view St Martins church stay on this road, and take a left after a short while to get to the church. Otherwise, 40 yards after passing the chippy turn left on to Cliff Bottom to go steeply uphill, staying to the left at an immediate fork in the road.

After around 150 yards, just after a car parking area go through a gate on the left to go in to a field. Immediately, the path here starts to climb steeply but keeps in the same direction crossing a number of fields, and passing the famous Boundary Stone until it reaches houses on the edge of Eyam village. Here it becomes a track, and then joins up with Mill Lane coming from the right and is then a tarmacced road which leads down into the village.

After passing the Lydgate graves on the left, the road reaches the village centre which is a good spot to have a cuppa and read the various information boards. From here, turn right to take the road uphill, passing Eyam Tearooms on the right. Stay on this road, then opposite the last house on the right, cross the road to go up Riley Lane. After quarter of a mile fork right, then after passing the Riley Graves on the left in another quarter of a mile, the entrance to Riley House Farm is reached. Take the path on the right here to enter woods passing a disused quarry area on the left. After about 200 yards the path bends left to go down a short banking and then meets cross paths. Turn right here to go downhill on a path through the woods which further down becomes a track and then leaves the woods to become enclosed as it carries on downhill to reach a disused road.

Cross the road slightly left to go through a gate into a field, and head for the main road at the bottom of the hill. Cross the road on to the road opposite, to pass the grounds of Stoke Hall and enter the village of Froggatt. Turn right at the other side of the bridge, then after about 40 yards go through a gate on the right and on to the river path. Follow this path for half a mile until it reaches a road. Cross the road and turn right to reach the bend in the road. Ignoring the path left, go straight forward at the signpost on a path which immediately climbs a banking to the left, and then enters a field.

Straight ahead is a gate which heads towards the top left corner. Through this, go half left to a gate in the wall which is just below a derelict barn. Once through the gate walk up the next field staying close to the wall to reach woods at the top. Go over a stile in to the woods, then turn immediate left on to a path which stays next to the wall until it ends just before a large metal gate. Take the track which doubles back to the right, and stay on it as it leads down to the main road. Cross slightly right on to Donkey Lane, then take the next right, Sough Lane to return to the start.

Look out for…..

The Toll House which has an unusual octagonal shape and was designed to match St Martins church which is also octagonal. The house was built in 1840 and is said to be the only Grade 11 listed chippy in the country, and has been used as a fish and chip shop since 1926.

St. Martin's church which was built by Joan Eyre in the 15th Century in thanksgiving for the safe return of her husband from the Battle of Agincourt. It is a very unusual building. The octagonal nave (the oldest of only two in Britain) is very interesting as all the pews face the centre of the church focusing the attention of visitors to the middle of the church, rather than the front, creating an intimate feeling which is unique to this style of church.

The Boundary Stone was created during the 1665 Eyam plague to separate Eyam residents who had self- quarantined, from those from Stoney Middleton who weren't affected. The 6 holes were made in the stone for plague money to be placed in vinegar by Eyam residents, in exchange for food and medical supplies.

The Riley Graves are a memorial to the family of Elizabeth Hancock who buried her husband and six children in eight days in August 1666 at the height of the plague outbreak.

Stoke Hall has had many owners over the centuries; the first occupant of the estate being Gerbert de Stoke in 1204, although the present hall was built around 1757. It passed through the ownership of a succession of Sheffield businessmen during the last century before being turned into a hotel and restaurant for a while, although it has now reverted to being a private residence again. In the 19th century Stoke Hall was allegedly the scene of a murder when a servant called Flora was brutally killed there. Her employers erected a statue to her memory which was reputed to move positions in the woods whilst her ghost is said to haunt the hall. The 'Fair Flora' statue still stands in private woods.

Dog Suitability

This isn't a good walk for dogs to be off-lead due to the route passing through fields of sheep and villages, and also because of the road walking.

Refreshments

There are tea rooms and the Miners Arms in Eyam, plus the Moon Inn at Stoney Middleton, and the Eyre Arms and Derwentwater Arms at Calver.

Walk No 12 : Sheffield Lakeland

8 miles / 4.5 hours

Introduction

Sheffield Lakeland lies to the north west of Sheffield and further on in the chapter there are details about the 14 reservoirs of which it comprises, and also how Sheffield Lakeland got its name. The walk chosen for this book takes place in an area between Wharncliffe Side and High Bradfield, and early on in the route it passes next to two of Sheffield Lakelands reservoirs, More Hall and Broomhead. A lofty climb then leads to Rocher Edge high above Agden reservoir, where two more Bradfield reservoirs, Dale Dike and Strines can be seen. On a clear day, in the distance, are more reservoirs in the Upper Don Valley too. Other walk highlights include views down to Broomhead reservoir from Walker Edge, Agden and Strines reservoirs from Rocher Edge, the amazing Glen Howe park at Wharncliffe Side, and the history of High Bradfield. The route taken is through a mixture of woodland paths, field and reservoir tracks, and some road walking along a few quiet country roads.

Agden Reservoir looking down from Rocher Edge

START

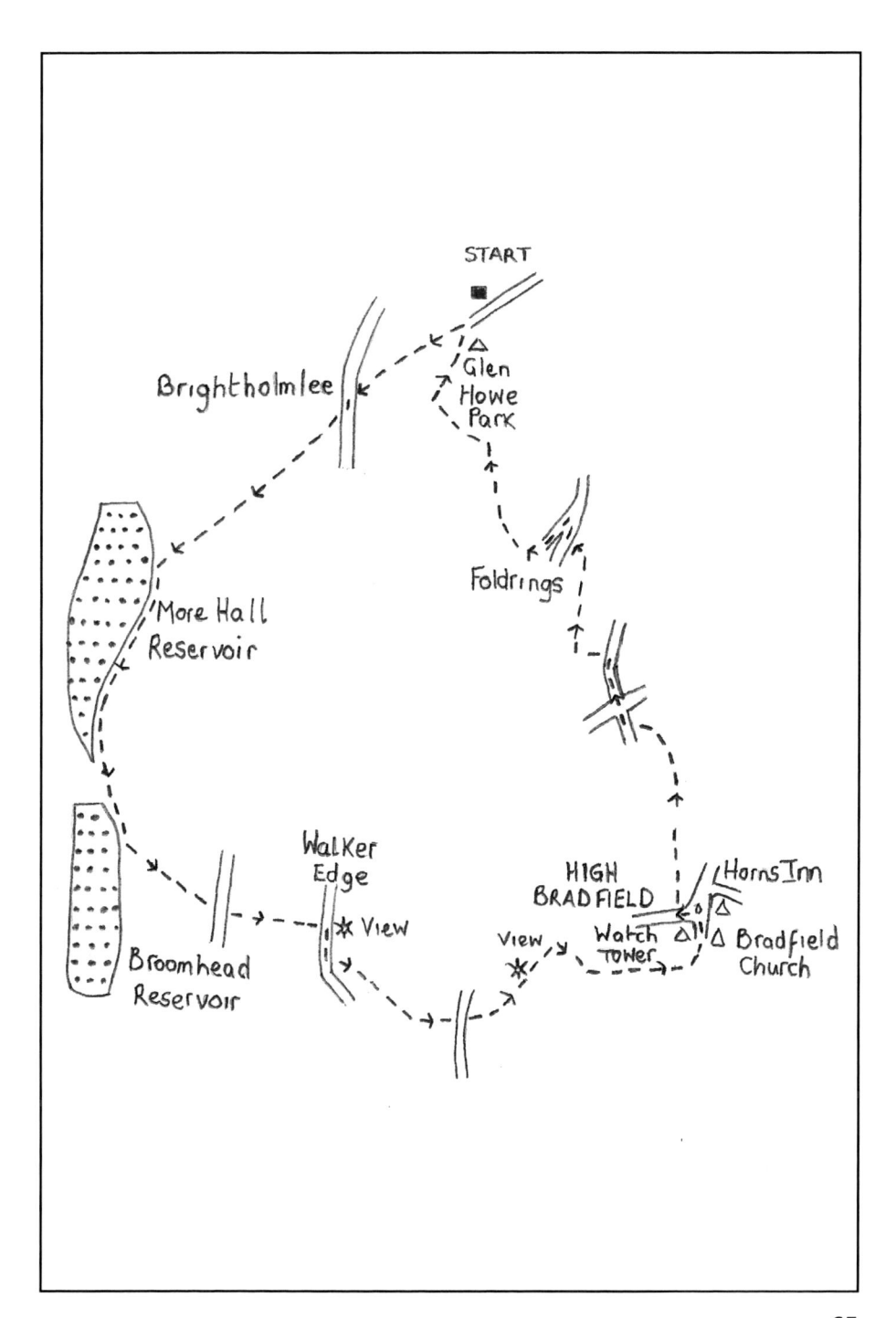

Brightholmlee

Glen Howe Park

More Hall Reservoir

Foldrings

Broomhead Reservoir

Walker Edge
* View

View *

HIGH BRADFIELD
Watch Tower

Horns Inn
Bradfield Church

65

Walk Difficulty

This is not an easy walk and includes a number of climbs, and quite a lot of stiles too. One woodland climb is very rocky, but the downhill sections of the walk aren't too difficult. As usual, expect a lot of mud in winter.

Starting Point

Glen Howe Park car park, Storth Lane, Wharncliffe Side, S35 0DW. What3Words: **grabs.silk.kicks**.

The Route

Turn right out of the car park and take the track uphill which after half a mile reaches Brightholmlee Lane. Turn left and take the 2nd path right between barns. At the end of the track cross a field into a wood which leads down to More Hall reservoir. Turn left on a wide path next to the reservoir and stay on this path until after ¾ of a mile it reaches a road. About 25 yards before this path reaches the road, go through a gate on the left to cross the road, straight on to another wide path which climbs up to Broomhead reservoir.

Once on the flat, after a couple of minutes take a path left to go up a few steps to enter woods. The next half a mile now consists of very strenuous uphill paths, crossing a road on the way up to reach Walker Edge. Turn right here and walk along the road for a quarter of mile, enjoying the views to the right, to then take a path on the left up a banking, just after the road has started to go downhill. This path stays to the left of a wall climbing steadily uphill then going along the edge of a wood to reach a country lane.

Cross the road on to a path through a sheep field which rises slightly, and bends left as it reaches the top of Rocher Edge. Stay on this path which has a steep drop to the right as it soon reaches a gate on the right. Go through the gate to keep in the same direction with a wall on the left. Further on, as the path drops down a short banking it is joined by a green lane coming up from the right. For a short while there is a banking on the left and woods on the right until the lane bends right to go into the trees, passing the top of a stream. Out of the woods the lane bends left to head towards a road, but on this bend take a path right which goes through a field with trees to the right.

Stay on this path which draws closer to a wall on the left as it drops downhill, finally meeting the wall at the bottom of the hill where there is a path going left and right. Turn right here to reach trees straight in front, then turn left to go downhill through the trees with a stream to the right. At the bottom of the hill there is a crossroad of paths with a small bridge on the right. Go left and stay on this path as it bends right and then climbs with a steep drop to the right, as it heads towards Bradfield Church. At the top of the hill cross another path to go through the churchyard to reach Jane Street.

To go to the Horns Inn turn right, and it is 50 yards along this street. To carry on with the walk turn left to go up Jane Street to Brown House Lane. Turn left, then cross the road to take an immediate path right which passes through trees initially, then goes through a field to the left of a wall. The path carries on for half a mile in roughly the same direction crossing fields until it reaches Delf Road. After crossing the road cross more fields on an obvious path, again keeping in roughly the same direction, to reach Onesacre Road.

Turn right along the road, go straight on at the crossroads, then take a path left after 1/3rd of a mile leading to a farm. The path bears right to pass above the farm and crosses a farm track staying to the edge of a field as it heads towards woods. Cross a stile to enter the woods on to a narrow path which heads downhill to emerge on to Raynor Sike Lane next to a house. Turn right, then after 200 yards take a path left which is also a drive to houses. This little hamlet is called Foldrings. After passing the last house, with farm buildings ahead, take a path right. Go through two fields, then just after passing a stile on the left, at a third field go half right to head towards trees. Go through an opening in the trees further down, to enter Glen Howe Park.

At this point, there are various ways of getting back to the car park via a number of paths which crisscross. As long as a path is taken which goes downhill, and stays close to one of the two streams, then the car park will be reached at the bottom of the park. The route chosen for this walk is to enter the woods as described above, and then after a few yards to turn right at a 'T' junction. At the next 'T' go left to cross a bridge, then at the next 'T' go right to reach a fourth 'T' next to a large shelter on the right. Go left here and stay on this path until it reaches an old stone bridge. Turn right before the bridge on to a path which stays to the right of a stream to return to the car park.

Look out for…..

Sheffield Lakeland has fourteen reservoirs which are More Hall, Broomhead, Underbank, Langsett, Midhope, three at Redmires, two at Rivelin, Strines, Dale Dyke, Agden and Dam Flask. Having all these reservoirs so close together inspired Sheffield Corporation to run tours from the city centre in the 1950's to 'Sheffield Lakeland'. The recently-formed Sheffield Lakeland Landscape Partnership is an organisation funded by the National Lottery Heritage Fund as part of its national landscape partnerships programme to manage the landscape for the benefit of all.

Glen Howe Park is fascinating and a quirky sort of place with a selection of good trails, delightful streams bordered by rocks and ferns, a forest winding down through the park, an old packhorse bridge, a couple of sculptures, and a large drystone wall sculpture high up on the edge of the park.

St Nicholas Church at High Bradfield, which is Gothic Perpendicular in style and dates from the 1480s. There is evidence of an earlier church having been on the site, and there is an Anglo Saxon cross inside.

The Watch Tower at the bottom of Jane Lane. It was built in 1745 to allow relatives of the deceased to watch over the graveyard and apprehend body snatchers. In the 18th century, newly buried bodies risked being disinterred to be sold to medical schools for the study of anatomy.

Dog Suitability

For a lot of the walk, especially the first half, this is a good walk for dogs to be off-lead. After leaving High Bradfield there is a lot of field walking, and there could be sheep or cows in some of the fields.

Refreshments

In Wharncliffe Side, about half a mile from the start of the walk are a shop, and The Blue Ball pub. The Old Horns in the centre of High Bradfield is passed on the route and has great views over Loxley Valley from its beer garden.

Walk No 13 : Carsington Water

8 miles / 4 hours

Introduction

Carsington Water is the ninth largest reservoir in the country and was opened in 1992. After it was built, Severn Trent Water created a path round the reservoir, and this route takes advantage of this path, as well as including a short diversion to take a look at the picturesque old mining villages of Carsington and Hopton. The Visitors Centre where the walk starts from is a tourist attraction in its own right, and is well worth spending some time at, especially Stones Island; and there is also a Sculpture Trail and Hob's Trail to watch out for whilst walking round the reservoir. The path round the reservoir is mainly flat, and there are no great inclines and no stiles whatsoever, making this a fairly easy eight miler.

Summer sailing on the reservoir

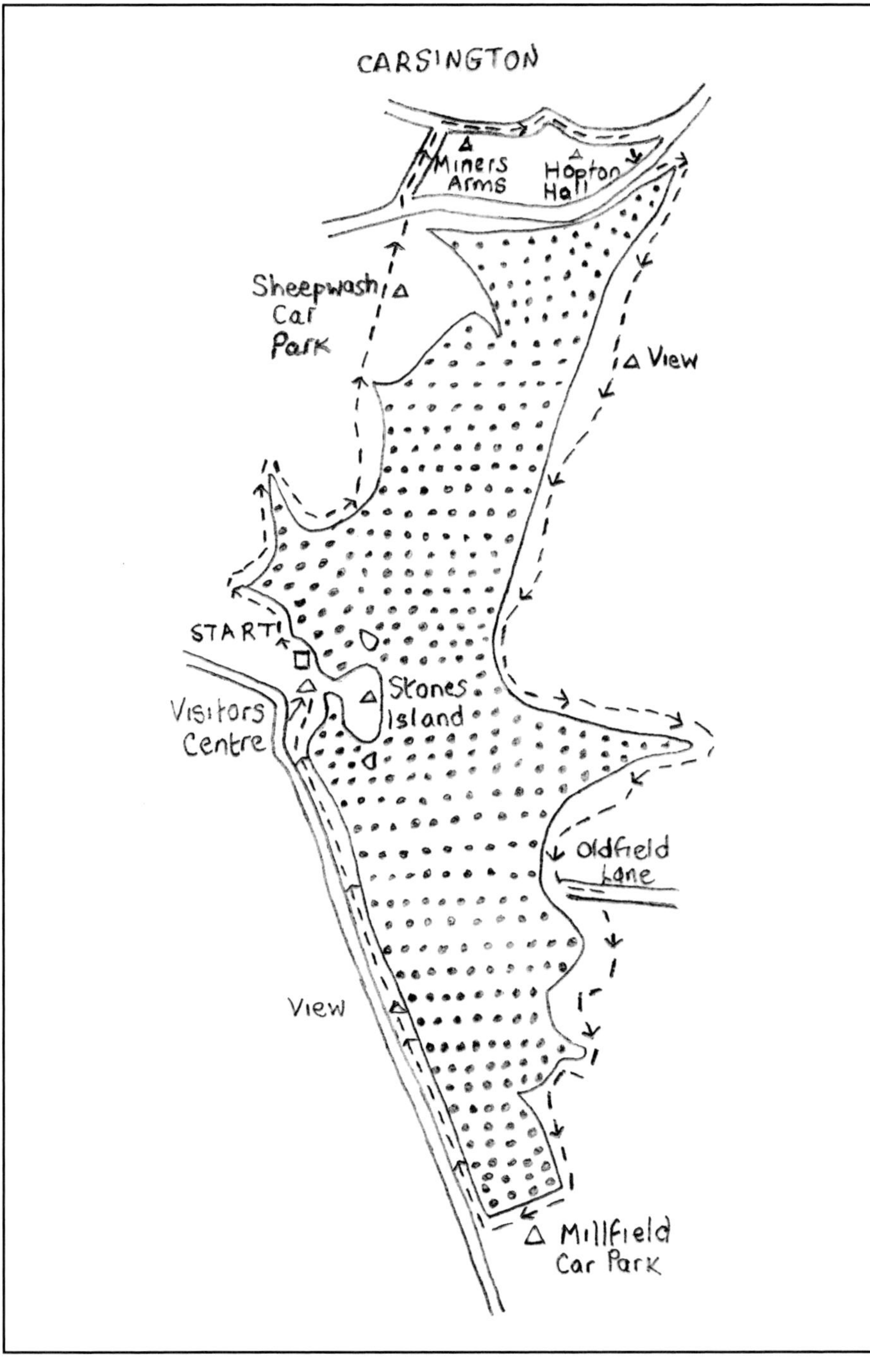

CARSINGTON
Miners Arms
Hopton Hall
Sheepwash Car Park
View
START
Stones Island
Visitors Centre
Oldfield Lane
View
Millfield Car Park

Walk Difficulty

There is nothing difficult at all about this walk. It is suitable for all levels.

Starting Point

Carsington Water Visitor Centre, Big Lane, Upper Town, Ashbourne DE6 1ST. What3Words: **headers.stays.crucially.** The walk could also be started from Sheepwash or Millfield car parks where parking fees are slightly cheaper.

The Route

Facing the visitors centre, take the path to the left which leads away from the centre around the outside of the car park. Where the car park ends the path turns right to go round the reservoir. After meandering round a few bends, after almost a mile and a half the path reaches Sheepwash car park. Leave the path here to walk along the road into the car park to reach the main road. Go left, then cross the road to take the road on the right which leads in to Carsington village.

At the 'T' junction in the village go right, then stay left to go above the pub to walk along the main road through the village. Further on, the road enters Hopton and passes Hopton Hall before passing through the village itself. After the last house on the right take a path next to it which leads down to the main road again. Cross the road and turn left on to the reservoir path which immediately bends right to reach the opposite side of the water.

From here, the path stays close to the water for about two and a half miles until it reaches Oldfield Lane. Turn left here to walk up the lane past holiday cottages, then after a minute or two, take a path right to carry on with the circuit round the water. After another mile the path reaches Millfield car park where there are toilets and a refreshment kiosk. Take the path here which leaves the car park to the right to carry on back to the starting point.

Look out for…..

The Sculpture Trail which was created to encourage visitors to interact with nature, and learn more about the local landscape. There are eight wooden sculptures at roughly every mile round the reservoir. Look out also for Hob's Trail which is themed round fairytales.

Carsington village dates back to prehistoric times with remains of a woolly rhino having been found in the village 20 years ago. Roman remains have also been found there including 3c glassware and evidence of an underfloor heating system at the site of a Roman Villa.

Hopton almshouses were built in 1722 and above them a stone tablet declares that the buildings were for '2 poor men and 2 poor women of Hopton and Carson', the latter being the old name for Carsington.

Hopton Hall is a magnificent country house: Elizabethan in origin, but largely Georgian in appearance.

Stones Island erected in 1992, is a short stroll from the visitor centre. It follows in the long tradition in Derbyshire of hill-top monuments. The objectives of the site are, to present a notable feature within the landscape which when viewed from a distance and when reached, attracts attention back to the surrounding countryside. Holes have been pierced in each of the stones to enable visitors to focus on particular features rather than just on the area as a whole. The heights of the holes have been varied so that small children can enjoy the experience.

Dog Suitability

This is a great walk for dogs. The path all the way round Carsington Water is enclosed, although there are sheep in some nearby fields to it. Dogs must be lead of course on the road through Carsington and Hopton villages.

Refreshments

There is a restaurant and a food kiosk at the visitors centre, and a seasonally open kiosk at Millfield on the other side of the reservoir. The Miners Arms in Carsington and the Knockerdown Inn are both very welcoming pubs.

Walk No 14 : Birley Edge

5.25 miles / 2.5-3 hours

Introduction

This is a fairly easy walk which has quite a good variety of scenery. Starting from close to the River Don, to start with the walk heads off through Beeley Wood and across farmland to reach Back Edge, climbing steadily all the way. Still climbing, the views over the Don Valley open up as Back Edge rolls into Birley Edge, and a lovely section full of gorse, bilberry bushes, heather and silver birch trees. After passing Jaw Bone Hill, the route reaches Wharncliffe Woods and crosses over the Barnsley border for a short while before it leaves the woods to enter an old industrial site close to Oughtibridge. After heading down into the centre of Oughtibridge the walk follows a really nice stretch of the River Don to return to the start..

The River Don at Oughtibridge

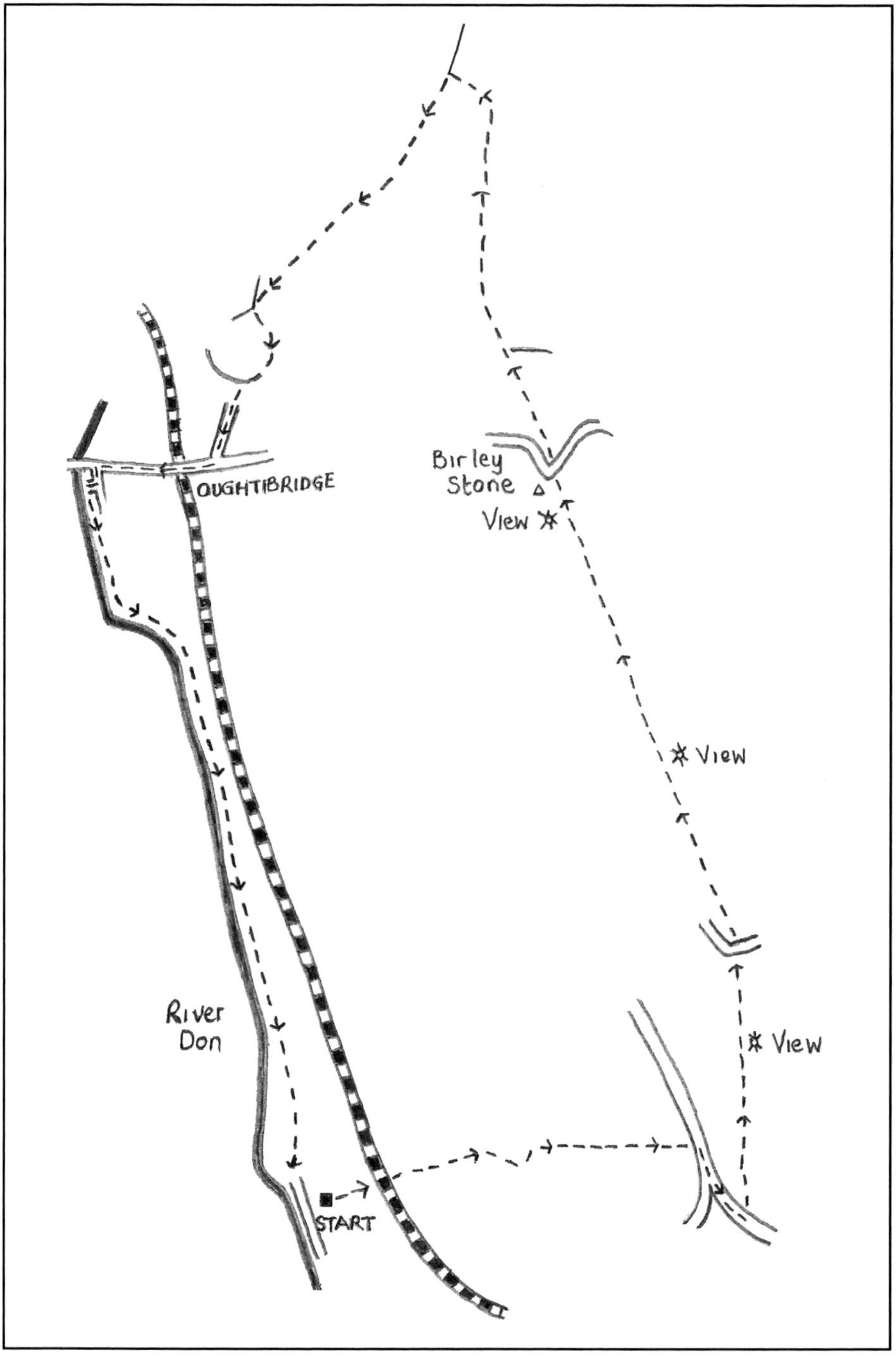
Birley
Stone
View
OUGHTIBRIDGE
View
River
Don
View
START

Walk Difficulty

Anyone who can walk 5 miles or more shouldn't have a problem with this walk. There is the steady half hour climb in the first part of the walk, but the paths are pretty good, and of course there could be the usual mud in winter.

Starting Point

The walk starts at the end of Beeley Wood Lane, S6 1ND, which is the address for Abbey Forged Products, also situated at the end of the lane. There is roadside parking next to the starting point. What3Words: **sank.bonus.sends.** The walk could also be started in the centre of Oughtibridge.

The Route

From Abbey Forged Products walk back along the lane for a few yards to take the second path left which leads uphill into woods with a wire fence on the right. After crossing over a railway bridge turn immediate right to head towards fields. Go through two fields to then walk along a green lane towards Underhill Farm. After passing through a gap stile pass the first farmhouse then just before the second one turn left on to a vehicle turn round area. There is a path here in the top right corner between bushes which is a little hard to find. Once through the bushes the path enters a field.

Turn right to find a signpost on the right indicating that the path goes uphill across a field on the left, passing above an electricity pylon. At the top of the field go over a stile into another field. After 30 yards go through a wall on the right to aim for a signpost at the top of the next field. Over the stile, stay to the left of the next field as the path heads towards Midhurst Road. Turn right along the road, and when another road joins from the right keep in the same direction. Take the second path on the left, on the brow of the hill on to a path which passes to the left of a new housing estate on its way to Back Edge.

The path stays on the top of Back Edge with far-reaching views until it reaches Edge Lane. Cross the road on to Birley Edge to carry on in the same direction to then reach Oughtibridge Lane at a point known locally as Jaw Bone Hill. Across the lane the path still remains high up and further on enters Wharncliffe Woods at a stile.

Over the stile take the left path to descend through the woods. After half a mile of twisting and turning and gradually descending, the path reaches a track just after crossing a stream. Go left to continue downhill for three quarters of a mile, then fork left on to another track which carries on downhill. Very soon, the path bends to the right, and a hut can be seen on the left, with a house just behind it. Leave the track here on to a path which passes between the hut and the house and stay on it as it bends left to leave the woods on to a works road. When this road reaches the main road turn right to go downhill to Oughtibridge. Opposite the entrance to the park cross the road to take the road opposite, Waterside Gardens. After 25 yards go right, then at the river turn left to walk alongside the river back to the start.

Look out for…..

The Birley Stone. At the top of Jawbone Hill there is a viewing area where you can find the Birley Stone which dates from 1161. Next to it sits the Festival Stone, erected in 1951 to commemorate the Festival of Britain. The Festival stone is a toposcope indicating notable features and landmarks which can be seen across the Don Valley.

Oughtibridge whose origins date back to the first part of the 12th century when a ford existed at the River Don. The ford was managed by a man named Oughtred who lived in a nearby cottage. When a bridge was built on the spot in approximately 1150 it became known as Oughtred's Bridge or by his nickname of Oughty's Bridge, and the small settlement around the bridge adapted the same name and eventually it became known as Oughtibridge.

Dog Suitability

Most of this walk takes place in woods or on top of the edges, which are perfect for dogs to be off-lead. There are just a couple of fields where there might be animals, and there is also a small amount of road walking.

Refreshments

There are a number of pubs, shops and takeaways in Oughtibridge for refreshments including The Pheasant inn which is passed en route.

Walk No 15 : Shillito Wood

4.75 miles / 2.5 hours

Introduction

This is a fascinating walk and covers several different landscapes and includes various ancient landmarks. Stone crosses, a bronze age stone circle, old waterworks and reservoirs are all passed as the route leads through woods and moorland. There may also be the possibility of spotting red deer on Big Moor too. The walk starts at Shillito Wood and uses ancient packhorse routes and moorland tracks to take place entirely within the Eastern Moors, part of the Dark Peak section of the Peak District. There are far-reaching views to enjoy across Big Moor which is crossed after passing through Ramsley Moor at the start of the walk.

13c Stone Cross in Shillito Wood

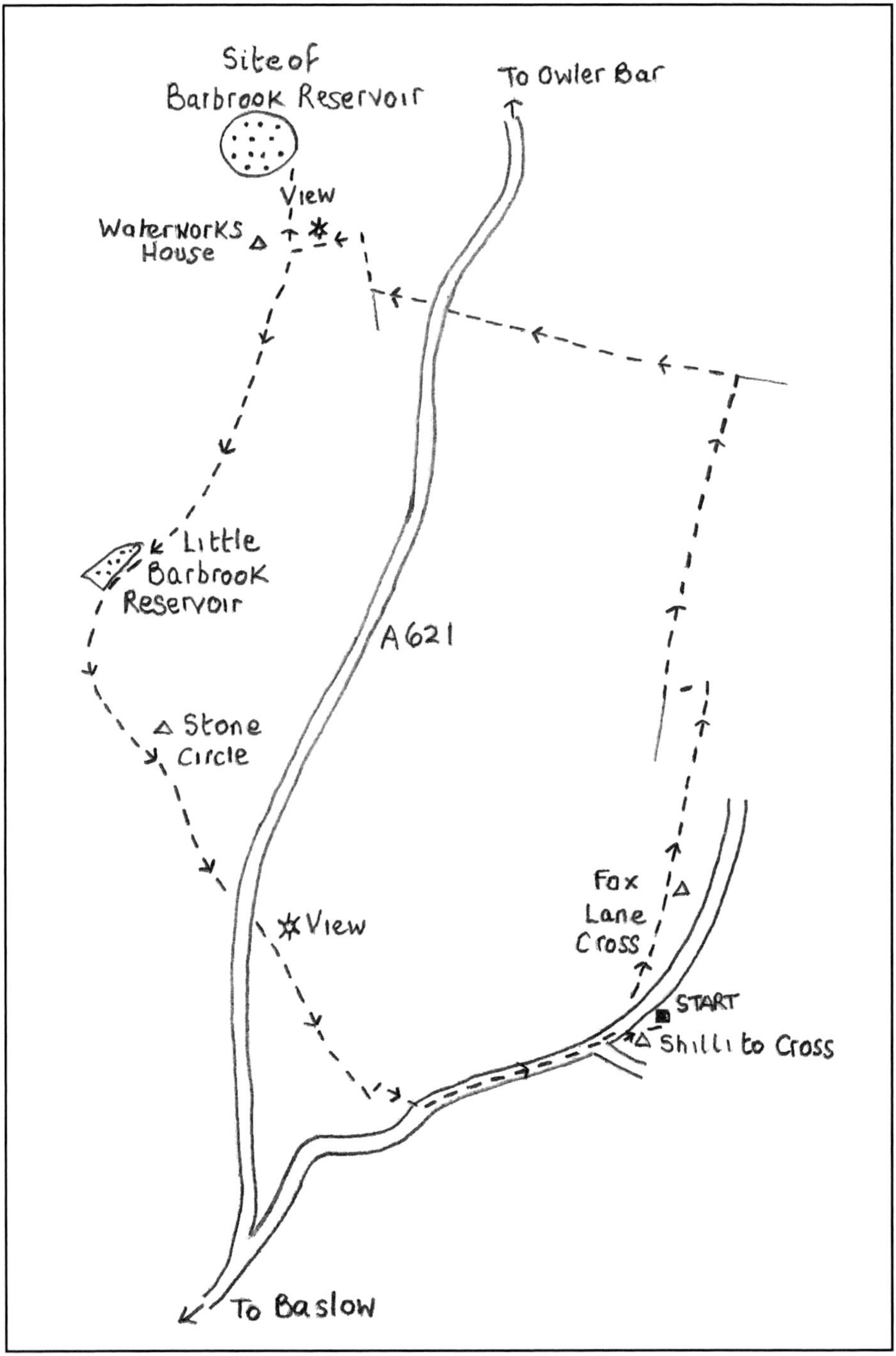

Site of Barbrook Reservoir
To Owler Bar
View
Waterworks House
Little Barbrook Reservoir
A621
Stone Circle
View
Fox Lane Cross
START
Shillito Cross
To Baslow

Walk Difficulty

Parts of the route can get muddy in winter or after heavy rain, and there is a long, rocky climb of about half a mile to negotiate.

Starting Point

Shillito Wood car park at Fox Lane, situated a mile from the A621 near Clodhall Lane. There is no postcode for the car park but What3words: **shelf.rail.lyricism** will take you straight there.

The Route

Cross the road to a gate opposite the car park. Through the gate go right to take a path right which to start with stays parallel to the road. Stay on this path as it passes through another gate and then moves away from the road, and heads in the direction of a stone cross in the distance. Bear left at the cross as the path drops down to meet a wire fence on the left, then stay next to the fence to reach a gate in the corner. Go through the gate on to a narrow path which stays next to a barbed wire fence as it drops steeply downhill.

At the bottom of this path, once through another gate turn right on to a wide path which goes through woods, and tracks a stream for quite a while before crossing it to reach Car Road, an old packhorse route. Go left up the rocky Car Road to the main road, then cross it to go through a gate at the other side. Go straight forward on to a feint path leading uphill to soon reach a path 'T' junction. Go right on to a grass track which meets a tarmac drive further up. Go left along the drive, then just before an ex-Waterworks house ahead, either turn right to go up a track to view the site of the old reservoir a few minutes away, or take a wide path on the left leading away from the house.

Keep on this path as it leads towards Little Barbrook Reservoir, passing to the left of it. Further on, just after the path bends to the left it passes a Stone Circle on the left which is worth a quick detour. Back on the path keep in the same direction to reach the main road. Cross the road to go through a gate to the right leading on to a grass track. At the end of the track ignore a path right to go through a gate on to a path above a small reservoir on the left.

At the road, cross and then turn left to walk along the road towards Shillito Wood. After crossing a road on the right, take a path on the right into the woods and immediately bear left on to a path which heads up to a wall at the top of the woods. Go left at the wall on to a bridle track, and after passing Shillito Stone Cross on the left the path leads directly back to the car park.

Look out for.....

Shillito Cross which was erected by monks from Beauchief Abbey in Sheffield in the 13c. Crosses were set up as waymarkers, preaching crosses or sometimes to establish the boundaries of lands owned by different abbeys.

Fox Lane Cross is a well-preserved example of a simple wayside cross set in its original location on a route across open moorland. It is unusual in that it includes an integral shaft and cross head but is generally similar in appearance to its partner, Shillito Cross on the opposite side of Fox Lane.

Upper Barbrook Reservoir was constructed in 1882 by the Chesterfield Union Water Works. In 1910 a new dam wall was constructed enabling the dam to hold 100 million gallons. Late in the 20c it ceased to be used, and all that is left now is a giant puddle. **Little Barbrook Reservoir** further down the valley was used as part of the Chesterfield water collection and distribution system. Nowadays it is a popular spot for wild swimming.

Barbrook Stone Circle is thought to be from the Bronze age (2000-700BC) and is a mecca for the people wanting to gather at the winter solstice. The cairn to the north of it is possibly a burial chamber.

Dog Suitability

The first half of the walk is perfectly suitable for dogs to be off-lead, but on Big Moor there could be sheep, so dogs need to be kept under close control.

Refreshments

A short drive away are The Royal Oak at Millthorpe, The Peacock at Owler Bar, and various pubs and cafes at Baslow.

Walk No 16 : Victorian Sheffield

5.25 miles / 2.5 hours

Introduction

In suburbs close to the centre of Sheffield is evidence of the wealth generated by the Victorian entrepreneurs who made their money from the Industrial Revolution. From the imposing houses in the Tapton area to parks and gardens created from their wealth, there are hidden gems to discover throughout this walk. The walk created here links together some of the parks and gardens created in the 19th century by walking through Victorian streets and gennels which were common to this era. In total there are three parks, two gardens and also the General Cemetery included in the route, as well as an old snuff mill and a fairly recently discovered "lost" garden. Some great old landmarks such as Broombank House, Botanical Gardens and Weston Park are passed on the route and if never visited before, time needs to be taken to investigate these places.

Tapton Walk, a well-preserved 19c gennel

82

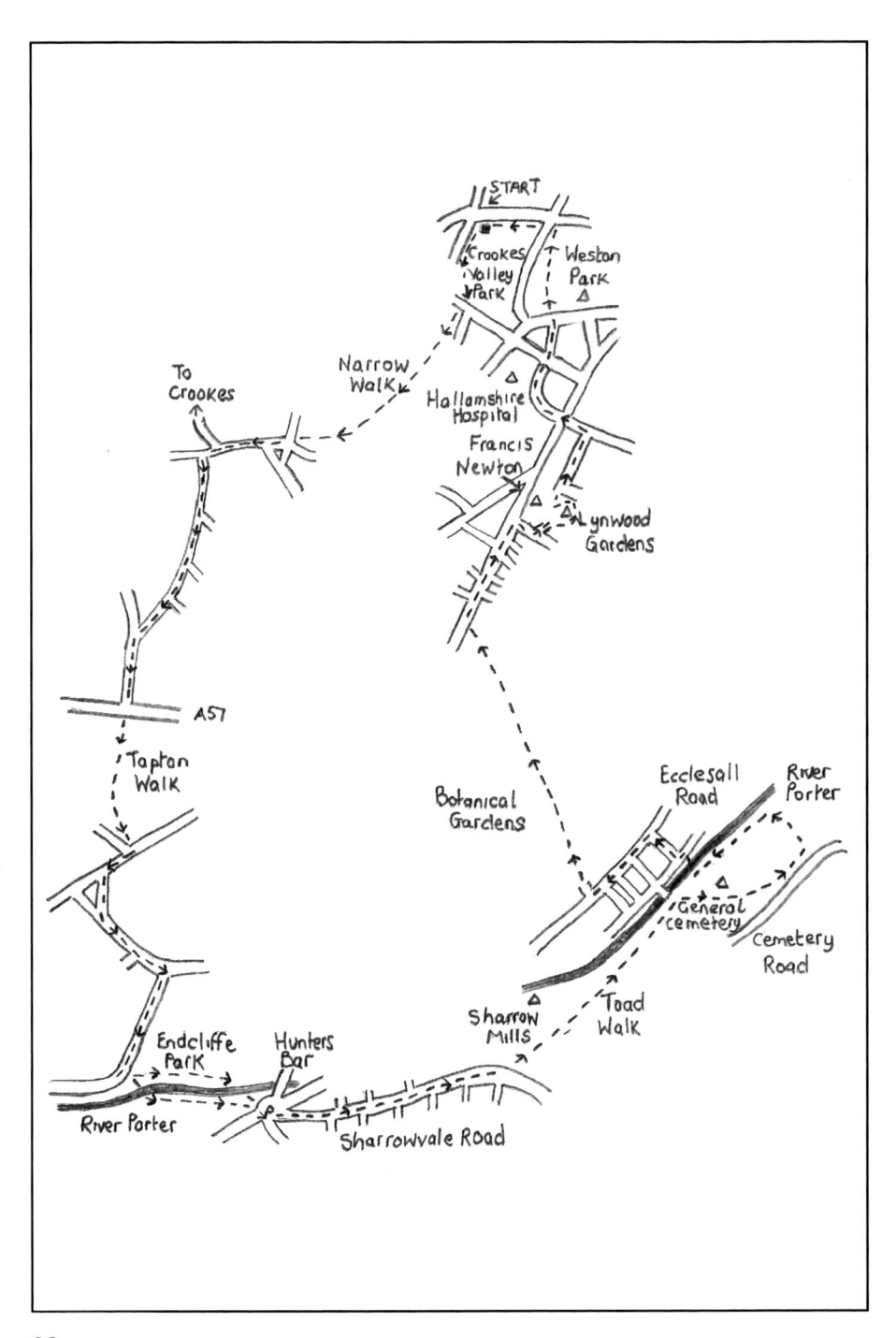

Walk Difficulty

There is nothing difficult about this walk at all, and no boots are required!

Starting Point

As there is currently free unrestricted on-street parking on Oxford Street, and other streets to the north of Crookes Valley Road, the starting point for this route is the entrance to Crookes Valley Dam on the corner of Crookes Valley Road and Harcourt Road. What3Words: **maker.pull.works**. If preferred, the walk could be started anywhere within the route though.

The Route

From the entrance to Crookes Valley Park go down steps into the park to walk along the right-hand side of the dam. As the path leaves the park on to a drive go right for a few yards towards a small car park, then take metal stairs on the left which lead to a wide path/drive between university sports buildings. When the path comes out on to Northumberland Road, cross to a gennel (Narrow Walk) slightly to the right. The path leads uphill to reach Crookesmoor Road. Cross on to Roslin Road opposite, which carries on uphill to Crookes Road. Cross the road to keep in the same direction, then after a few minutes, as Crookes Road bends right, go straight forward on to Lydgate Lane, then take the next left on to Hallamgate Road.

After ¼ mile Hallamgate Road joins Tapton House Road to stay in the same direction, dropping down on to Manchester Road. Straight opposite, take another gennel (Tapton Walk) which leads down to Fulwood Road. Cross the road and turn right, then take the next left, Woodvale Road. Down the hill, it joins Endcliffe Vale Road coming from the right. Cross the road here, then take the second right, Riverdale Road. Where Riverdale Road bends right, take a path on the left which leads into Endcliffe Park.

There is immediately a choice of paths which can be taken here. Either go down the steps ahead, then cross the river and turn left to pass the café and toilets, or go left to miss a pretty crowded part of the park. Either left or right, stay close to the river to leave the park at Hunters Bar. Turn right here, then cross Ecclesall Road at the crossing.

At the other side turn left and cross Junction Road to walk along Sharrowvale. After 1/3 a mile, just after the Jaguar dealer, go down a gennel (Toad Walk) on the left. At the bottom cross the Porter Brook then after a few yards turn right to enter the General Cemetery. Through the archway, stay on the main path as it climbs up towards the chapel, and then bends right towards the road. Just past the chapel take a path left to stay on the perimeter of the cemetery. Stay on this path staying close to two roads as it goes back downhill and bends to the left twice to head back towards the cemetery entrance. 200 yards along the bottom part of the cemetery grounds look for a path on the right which leads to a bridge over the Porter Brook. At the other side go left and stay on the path as it reaches Stalker Lees Road.

Turn left, then take any of the first 4 roads on the right which all lead to Ecclesall Road. Cross Ecclesall Road to go left, then take Thompson Road right to head towards the Botanical Gardens. Take any route up the gardens, but leave them by the gatehouse entrance at the top to go on to Clarkehouse Road. Turn right to walk along the road for 500 yards then turn right on to Park Lane, almost opposite King Edwards school swimming pool. About 100 yards along the road go left on to a narrow lane, Park Crescent which leads to Lynwood Gardens. In the gardens, stay right to walk round the pond then as the path bends left, take a path on the right which goes uphill slightly to a 'T'. Go right on to a path which leaves the gardens on to Dorset Road.

At the end of the road turn left to walk up Broomspring Lane to Glossop Road. Cross on to Claremont Place and stay on this road as it bends right and crosses Northumberland Road to reach Western Bank. Cross the road to enter Weston Park and walk through the park and leave it by the bottom entrance on the left. Turn left to cross Mushroom Lane to enter Crookes Valley Park, and stay to the right to return to the start.

Look out for…..

Crookes Valley Park and **Crookes Valley Dam**. The dam was originally known as The Great Old Dam and was built in 1785, along with 9 other reservoirs in the area to be the sole supply of water for the city of Sheffield. By the 20c none of the reservoirs were needed, and the other 9 were filled in.

Narrow Walk ran along the side of one of the above-mentioned reservoirs

Tapton Walk which was an extension of Tapton House Road in the 19c.

Sharrow Mills includes seven Grade II listed structures. These are the original 1763 snuff mill, the 1880 snuff mill, two bridges, stables, workshops and the dam walls of the mill pond.

Toad Walk is Sheffield dialect (t'owd walk)

General Cemetery information kindly provided by the Sheffield General Cemetery Trust. For more information regarding the amazing work carried out by this organisation see their website www.gencem.org

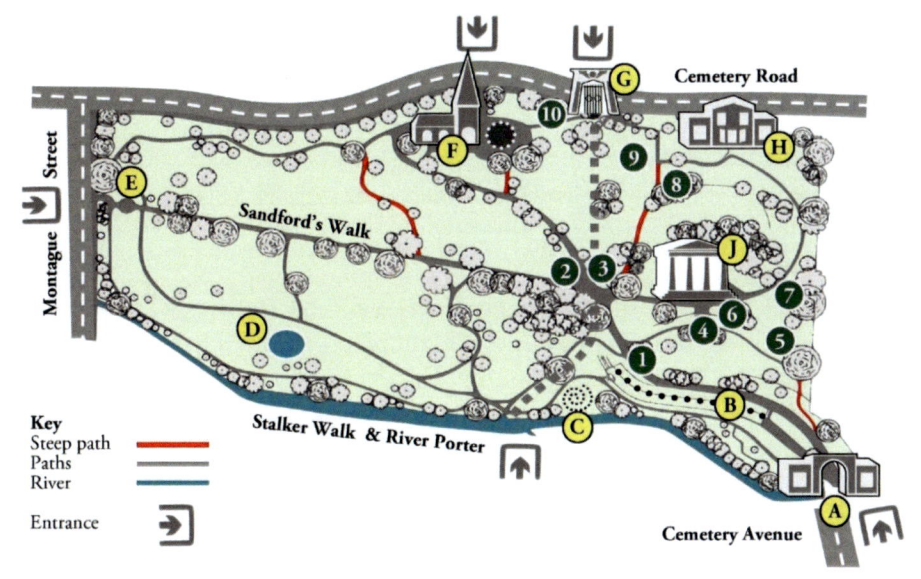

Monuments
1. John Cole - One of 3 brothers who founded Cole Brothers
2. Mark Firth - Steelmaster, Mayor, Master Cutler, Listed Grade II.
3. James Nicholson - Steelmaster. Listed Grade II.
4. George Bennet - Missionary, social reformer. Listed Grade II.
5. George Bassett - Sweet manufacturer, Alderman and Mayor.
6. Thomas Burch - Alderman, businessman.
7. William Parker - Merchant, businessman. Listed Grade II.
8. John Gunson - Engineer involved in Dale Dike Dam disaster 1864.
9. Samuel Holberry - Leading figure in the Chartist movement.
10. Ernest Shuttleworth - World War 1 serviceman

Buildings & Points of Interest

A. Gatehouse. Listed Grade II*. 1836.
B. Catacombs. Listed Grade II. 1836.
C. Stone Spiral. Educational. Used to demonstrate geology. 2004.
D. Wildlife Pond. Created by volunteers. 2018.
E. War Memorial. Erected here by the Commonwealth War Graves Commission 2015.
F. Anglican Chapel. Listed Grade II. 1850. Designed by William Flockton.
G. Egyptian Gate. Listed Grade II*. 1836. Ornamented with ancient symbols.
H. Original Cemetery office. Listed Grade II. 1836.
J. Samuel Worth Chapel. Listed Grade II*. 1836.

The Botanical Gardens were opened in 1836 and house over 5000 plants in its 19 acres. The gardens are listed by English Heritage as a Grade II site of special historic and architectural interest.

Broombank House re-named the Francis Newton by Wetherspoons in 2010, was built for the wealthy cutlery manufacturer Francis Newton, as his family home. The Georgian-style house was within easy walking or riding distance of his Portobello Works. In 1844, Newton was elected Master Cutler, the head of the prestigious Company of Cutlers.

Lynwood Gardens were part of Broombank House, and are a rare example of a Victorian garden which has remained virtually untouched for over 150 years. The garden was landscaped to mimic a Capability Brown Landscape in miniature, incorporating areas of mature trees within the garden.

Dog Suitability

Dogs need to be led for most of the walk, but in in the parks, and in Lynwood Gardens, dogs can be off-lead.

Refreshments

Endcliffe Park café, shops and cafes on Sharrowvale, the Curators House at Botanical Gardens and the Francis Newton pub are all en route

Walk No 17: White Edge Moor

8.5 miles / 4.5 hours

Introduction

The sheer vastness of White Edge Moor can be seen on this walk which crosses from one end of the moor to the other, and then returns to the start on a path above two more edges, Curbar and Froggatt. The walk also includes the Longshaw Estate including Longshaw Lodge, and the possibility of spotting wild deer throughout the walk. The route starts from the Fox House pub, just inside the Sheffield boundary, and apart from good paths through the Longshaw estate, is entirely then on paths and tracks through wild moorland. There are also far-reaching views of the Hope Valley, with Kinder Scout looming over it, and further views down towards the River Derwent and the Chatsworth Estate.

Looking towards Hope Valley from White Edge on a winters morning

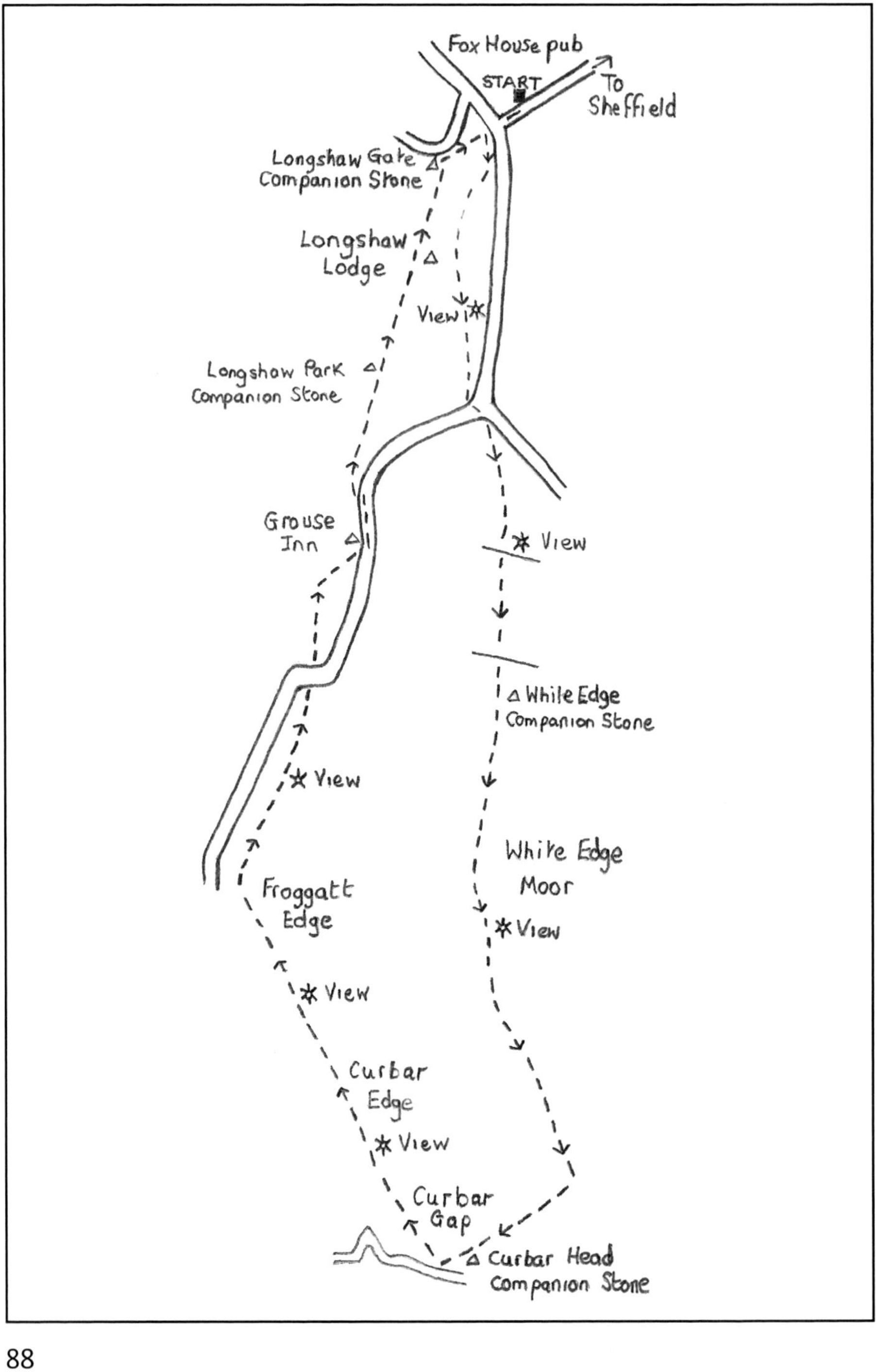
Fox House pub
START
To Sheffield
Longshaw Gate Companion Stone
Longshaw Lodge
View
Longshaw Park Companion Stone
Grouse Inn
View
White Edge Companion Stone
View
White Edge Moor
Froggatt Edge
View
View
Curbar Edge
View
Curbar Gap
Curbar Head Companion Stone

Walk Difficulty

There are no hills on this walk, just steady climbs which aren't too difficult, and there are no stiles to negotiate either. The terrain across the moor is very rocky though, and care must be taken there, and also alongside the steep drops on the edges. Mud and standing water are permanently on the moor in winter.

Starting Point

The walk starts at the Fox House pub, Hathersage Rd, Sheffield S11 7TY. There is a public car park next to the pub, or parking on Hathersage Road. What3Words: **copper.bump.brands**

The Route

Cross the road below the pub to go through a gate which leads into trees. Turn immediate left on to a path which meanders its' way through trees as it stays near to the road, crossing a car park entrance to reach a gate out of the wood. The path turns right here, with the woods now on the right until after a few minutes it is joined by another path coming out of the woods. Keeping in the same direction, the path has extensive views across the Longshaw Estate to the right as it heads towards a road at the top left corner.

At the road turn right, then at a road junction, cross over the island in the middle of the road. Go through a white five barred gate at the other side which leads on to a track. Immediately to the left are two wooden gates. Go through the one to the right then turn right to walk on a grass path next to a wire fence. After passing a small wood on the right the path reaches cross paths with a gate on the right. Go straight across on to a path which leaves the wire fence and heads towards White Edge.

After about half a mile, the path reaches more cross paths with a wall going left and right. Go straight forward here on to a path which is directly above White Edge. Stay on this path for two miles and then look for a signpost for Curbar Gap next to the corner of a wall. Go right here as directed by the signpost to head down steps towards Curbar Gap car park.

At the car park find a path in the top left-hand corner which leads into woods. The short path swings round to the right to join another path coming up from the left to pass through a gate leading to Curbar Edge. There are now two choices of paths, with the left one staying close to the edge and having great views on a clear day. Both paths join back up further on and as Curbar Edge becomes Froggatt Edge, the path stays close to the edges for 1.5 miles. Through a gate the path enters woods and stays in the trees for a further half a mile before it reaches a fork. Stay left, to quickly reach the main road. Turn right to walk along the road for 30 yards before crossing the road to go through a gate at the other side. Go down the steps to cross a stream, and then stay on the path as it passes a car park on the right.

Not long after passing the car park look for a gate on the right leading to a field. The path cuts through two fields to lead back to the main road. Turn left and walk along the road for a few minutes to go through a large white gate on the left to enter the Longshaw Estate again. The path here stays more or less in the same direction as it makes its way towards Longshaw Lodge. After just over a mile the path passes through two gates and goes past the front of the Lodge to join the Lodge drive. Walk along the drive almost to the end of it, then take a path on the right which leads up to the Fox House.

Look out for…..

Longshaw Lodge on the Longshaw Estate. Longshaw was once the Duke of Rutland's shooting estate, but was purchased from the Duke by public subscription in 1927 and presented to the National Trust. The estate stretches almost down to Grindleford and includes the area around Millstone Edge and the Burbage Valley, and is well known for the sheepdog trials which are held here every September.

Herds of Deer. Among other spectacular wildlife, White Edge Moor and Longshaw are home to a completely wild herd of around 170 red deer, the largest land mammal in the UK. Easily recognised by their magnificent antlers, stags (males) weigh in at up to 240kg and stand 1.3m high at the shoulder.

Companion Stones. On the Longshaw Estate there are three ancient guide posts known as stoops. Each stoop is accompanied by a 'companion stone', part of a 2010 art project. There are 12 companion posts in Derbyshire altogether, and one further one on this walk is at Curbar Head, making four Companion Stones in total to look out for on this walk. The location of the four Companion Stones is marked on the map of this walk. Here is what they say:

Longshaw Gate stone says, 'Come bye Look back Take time Walk on'.

Longshaw Park stone says, 'Walk on by water flow, by crow flight, by night, by star, by satellite, by map, by stone and so to home'.

Curbar Head stone says, 'Before the stone, before the land, the running hare, the pointing hand. The rattled wheel, the bright idea, something else, would lead us here.

White Edge stone says, 'For this ride, come outward. Hear heather on air step on grounded cloud. Let soul rotate as horizon walk skywards'

Boggarts of Longshaw. On the Longshaw Estate there exists a Boggart Trail, created for children. But what exactly is a Boggart? Here's an explanation, courtesy of Wikipedia *"A boggart can either be a household spirit or a malevolent genius who inhabits fields, marshes or other geographical features. The household form causes mischief and things to disappear, makes milk go sour, and dogs to go lame. The boggarts inhabiting marshes or holes in the ground are often attributed more serious evil doing, such as the abduction of children."*

Dog Suitability

There is the possibility of sheep for most of the walk, apart from in the middle of winter, so unfortunately this isn't really a dog-friendly walk.

Refreshments

The Fox House where the walk starts, and The Grouse Inn on the walk route are very popular pubs, and there is also the café at Longshaw Lodge for refreshments.

THE SCHOOLROOMS
cafe- gift & art shop

The perfect place to kick start your day in the Peaks, or, just take a break and enjoy a hearty meal!

www.theschoolrooms.co.uk
0114 2851 920
Mill Lee Road, Low Bradfield, Sheffield, S6 6LB

Walk No 18 : Limb and Porter Valleys

5.25 miles / 2.5 - 3 hours

Introduction

The Limb and Porter Valleys have long been associated with the industrial growth of Sheffield in the 18th and 19th centuries, and although the industry has all gone, the paths through the valleys are now important for another reason – as a way of getting Sheffield folk directly into the Peak District! In this easy-going walk, both upper parts of the valleys have been linked together with the use of field paths and old packhorse routes, with evidence of different parts of Sheffield's industrial and historical heritage being passed along the way. In fine weather, and at weekends and Bank Holidays, the paths up the valleys can be very busy, and quite rightly so, as apart from all the history, the surrounding countryside is within easy reach of many Sheffield people, and is quite stunning too.

Wintry scene at the derelict Copperas House which served Barber Fields mine at Ringinglow

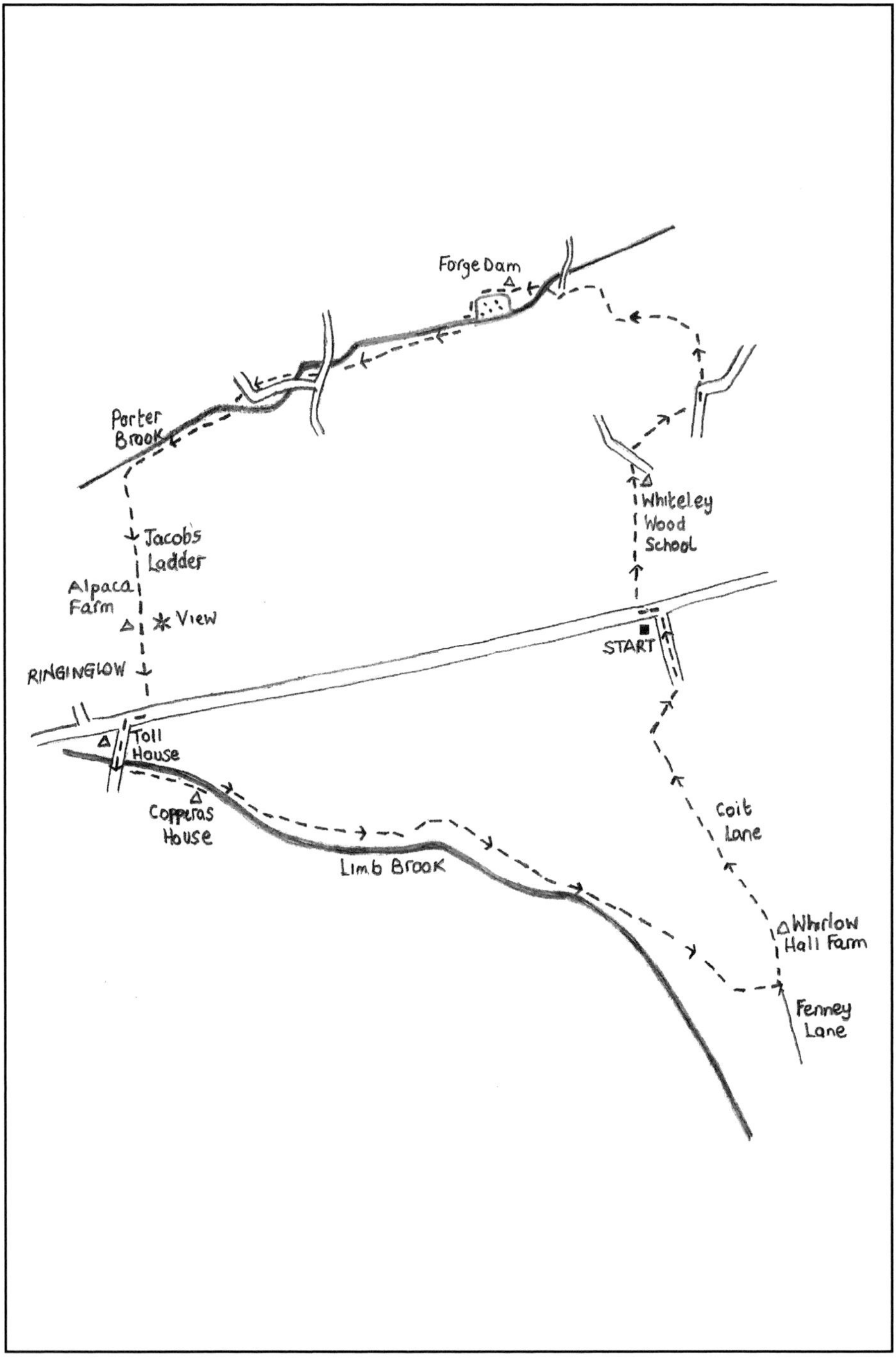
Forge Dam
Porter Brook
Jacobs Ladder
Alpaca Farm
View
RINGINGLOW
Toll House
Copperas House
Limb Brook
Whiteley Wood School
START
Coit Lane
Whirlow Hall Farm
Fenney Lane

Walk Difficulty

On mainly good paths and with just one short, sharp hill this is a fairly easy walk. In winter and after rain there could be a lot of mud though.

Starting Point

A small parking area on Ringinglow Road a few yards after the entrance to Birkdale School sports ground. Postcode for the sports ground is S11 7DB. What3words: **public.mole.bravo**. The walk could also be started at a car parking area further up Ringinglow Road, just before the crossroads.

The Route

From the parking area cross the road and turn left to walk up Ringinglow Road for a few yards, then take a footpath right. After passing an old school the path reaches Cottage Lane. Turn left, then after a few yards cross the road on to take a wide track known as Common Lane. At the end of the lane go left along the road for a few yards, and as the road bends right take the track on the left which drops down to a road opposite Forge Dam. Turn left, and then immediate right to reach the café area, and then go up the short steep path to the dam. Go to the right of the dam to cross a small bridge and then on to a path on the right which leads up the Porter Valley.

Stay on this path, keeping in the same direction, crossing a road as the path climbs steadily up the valley. At a second road go slightly to the left on to a track which carries on climbing in the same direction. After a few minutes, just before the track bends sharp right, go over a stile on the left on to a path which heads steeply up a field. This is Jacob's Ladder. At the top of the field go through a gate on to an enclosed path, with the Alpaca Farm on the right.

At Ringinglow Road, turn right and then after a minute or two turn left on to Sheephill Road. After the last house, go over a stile on the left on to an enclosed path signposted for Limb Valley. At the bottom of the field at the derelict building, take the second signpost on the right to go down steps on to a footpath at the head of the Limb Valley. From here, the path continues descending steadily, staying close to the Limb Brook, crossing it several times until after just under a mile it levels out.

At this point, a track leads across a bridge on the right towards Whirlow Hall. Ignore this, and instead carry on straight forwards for a couple of minutes before taking a path forking off to the left which leads uphill through trees. Out of the trees the path goes across a field to come out on to Fenney Lane, an enclosed old packhorse lane. Go left up the hill, to quickly reach Whirlow Farm. Cross over the farm track to keep in the same direction on to another enclosed lane, Coit Lane which eventually levels out as it leaves the woods. With a school sports field on the right the path bends round the field to reach a school building. Turn left to walk down the drive to return to the start.

Look out for…..

Whiteley Wood 'Open-air school' was established in 1909 by Sheffield City Council for children aged 10 and over suffering from serious illnesses who it was thought would benefit from having outdoor lessons. To start with lessons were held outside wherever possible, and there were other innovations such as breakfast provided, and the children were made to have a sleep after lunch in deckchairs with extended footrests, or on stretchers.

Porter Brook is one of Sheffield's 6 rivers, the others being the Don, Sheaf, Rivelin, Loxley and Limb Brook. Porter Brook descends over 1,000 feet from its source on Burbage Moor close to Ringinglow on its way in to the city centre. On the way down, there are dams which have served 19 water-wheels, which were mostly used for grinding corn, operating forge-hammers, and rolling mills, grinding knives and the various types of blade which made Sheffield famous.

Forge Dam has a recent claim to fame thanks to Jarvis Cocker who wrote the song *Wickerman* whilst he was sat at the dam. The dam was built by Thomas Boulsover in 1760 along with a lower dam, now filled in. Around the mid 1800's there were two water-wheels and a steam engine to power the forge's drop hammers. Forge Dam was sold in 1900 to a showman Henry Maxfield who used the dam as a boating pool for 20 years. 20 years later, Sheffield Corporation used the dam for boating until it became heavily silted.

Forge Dam cafe opened in the 1930s and the building is rumoured to have previously been Walkley Methodist Hall, until it was dismantled and brought on horse and cart to the park to be reassembled as the café.

Jacob's Ladder is a ladder leading to heaven which featured in a dream which Jacob had in the Book of Genesis in the bible. Subsequently the name 'Jacob's Ladder' has been given to dozens of steep hills all over the UK including a famous one on Kinder Scout. In the mid-20c Ringinglow's Jacob's Ladder was used as a ski slope when it snowed. In fact Hallamshire Ski Club used a portable tow rope as a type of ski lift on it when it snowed regularly.

Ringinglow is supposed to have got its name after a man lost on the moors in bad weather was saved when he heard the bells of Sheffield Parish Church 'ringing low' over the moors.

The Toll House at Ringinglow was built in 1758 and is a Grade ll listed building. Now a private residence, it was used as a shop in the mid 20c

Copperas House was part of Barber Fields mine, a small drift mine operated from the derelict building. It had a short railway track leading from behind the building up to a farm which is no longer there which was situated at the top of the field near the road. Winches and ponies were used to move the mine tubs along the railway. The mine was one of the nearest to the surface in South Yorkshire and it is said that footsteps and voices of people above ground could be heard by the miners who were working at the mine.

Herbert Trotter was the first owner of Barber Fields mine, and at the time the mine opened he lived at Fulwood, but pretty soon afterwards he had to move to Ringinglow to stop thieves stealing his coal. At the time, dozens of carts a day came across Houndkirk Road carrying goods such as Cheshire salt, iron ore, and lime from various places in Derbyshire for local farms. Coal was taken back in the opposite direction by the carters, and Trotter found that when he wasn't there, the carters stole his coal. First of all, he moved into a hut on the site, then later on he built a house nearby.

The Limb Brook rises in Ringinglow and flows in an easterly direction through Whirlow and Ecclesall Woods into the Beauchief area, where it merges with the River Sheaf. The brook has long been used as a source of power for local industry; remains of water-powered mills used for smelting lead and grinding corn can be seen further down the valley.

Fenney Lane, and **Coit Lane,** a continuation of Fenney Lane from above Whirlow Hall Farm, were busy thoroughfares from Derbyshire and Manchester into Sheffield well into the 19th century. Although Coit Lane now disappears into fields, the hedgerows suggest it must have once joined Ringinglow Road.

Whirlow Hall Farm has been the site of the Whirlow Hall Farm Trust, a registered charity which allows children and young people to visit a working farm since 1979. The site includes various Grade II listed buildings including Whirlow Farmhouse built on the site of the old Whirlow Hall. In the yard below the farmhouse is Whirlow Hall Cottage (sometimes called Low House) along with two ancient cruck barns and a cow shed.

Dog Suitability

This is a good walk for dog owners to have their dogs off-lead. Although there are nearby fields which have animals, there is only Jacob's Ladder field where there may be animals on the actual route. Care needs to be taken at the roads at the Porter Valley and passing through Whirlow Hall Farm though.

Refreshments

There are two excellent cafes passed on the route, Forge Dam in the Porter Valley, and Whirlow Hall Farm café.

Walk No 19 : Ford and Ridgeway

4.75 miles / 2.5 hours

Introduction

Straddling the Sheffield/Derbyshire border, this walk passes through beautiful unspoilt countryside, and some delightful hamlets and villages, in an area which also has an interesting industrial history. Starting from Ridgeway, the route uses mainly old packhorse routes and field tracks to start with, followed by a short amount of road walking through the lovely Sloade Lane area. After passing the interesting 17c Litfield Farm complex, farm tracks lead down to the 16c industrial hamlet of Birley Hay on the way to Ford, the halfway point of the walk. Picking up The Moss, a brook passing through Ford, paths now lead through the Moss Valley before turning sharply uphill through fields to Plumbley, for the return to start.

Mill Pond at Ford

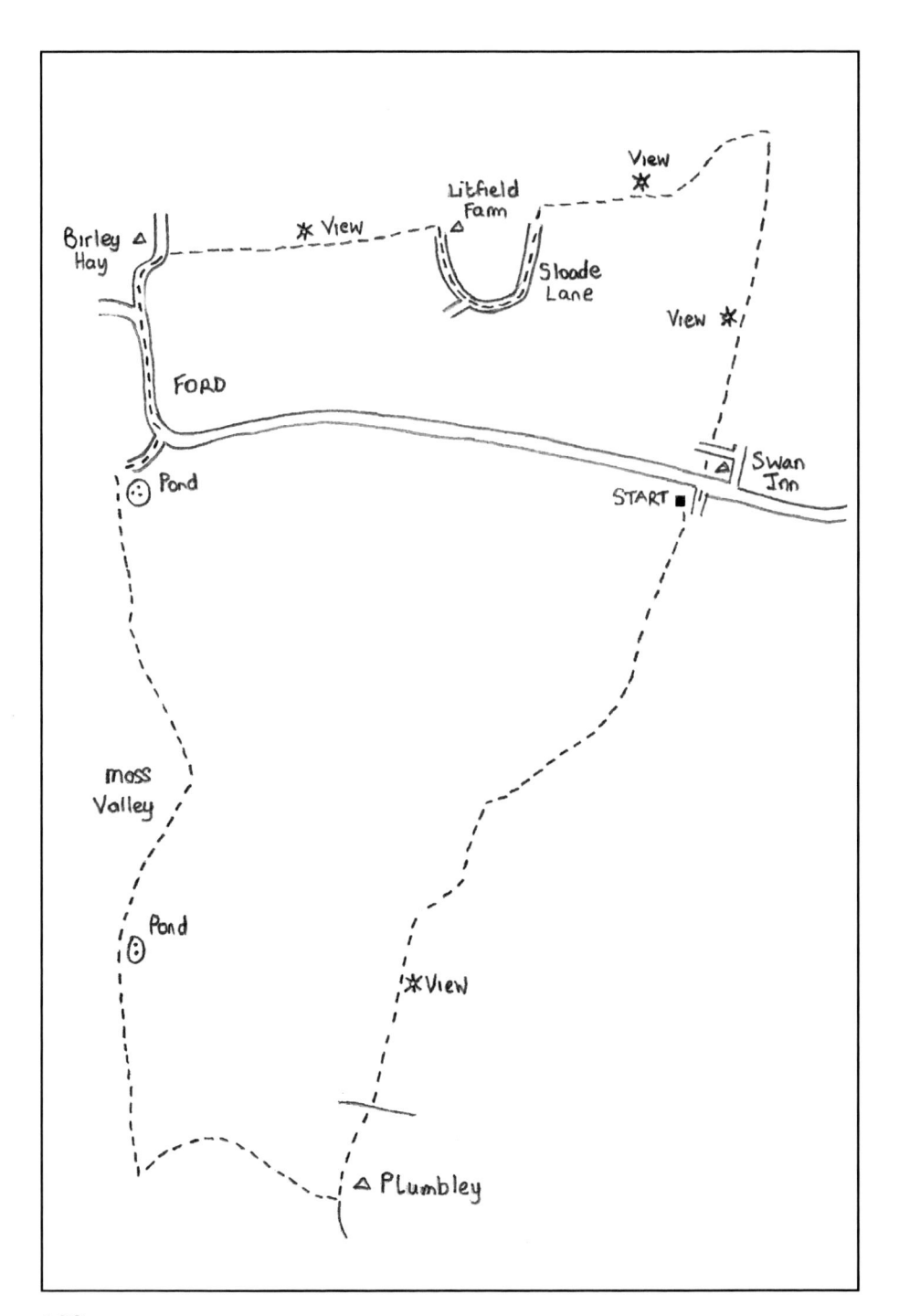

Walk Difficulty

Although there are a few short, sharp hills, and a number of stiles to negotiate, this is not a difficult walk although after rain, and in winter, there will be a few muddy sections to watch out for,

Starting Point

The public car park at Ridgeway Courtyard at Ridgeway. This is almost opposite The Swan Inn S12 3XR. What3words **local.fonts.trend** .

The Route

From the car park, return to the main road and cross to the Swan Inn. Take a path up the side of the pub which after crossing an estate road comes out into a field. Carry on to the top of the field where the path joins a track coming from the left, and stay in the same direction. After about 100 yards when the track bends right take a path on the left which leads downhill. At the bottom it is joined by a path coming from the left and stays in the same direction to go through a short, often muddy section to reach a bridge over a stream. At the other side, the path crosses a stile to go on to a partly paved enclosed section which leads uphill to reach a main path at the top. Turn left to soon go up a banking and through scrubland, At the top ignore a path right to go straight forward into a field. Cross this field, then in a second one head for the bottom corner to reach a path going left and right. Go left on a path which quickly becomes Sloade Lane. Stay on this road until it reaches a ford.

Turn right here to go uphill on a private road, Doe Lane. At the top of the lane head for the footpath sign, then turn left to walk along the edge of a field keeping to the right of a hedge. Into a second field the path drops down towards houses, still staying to the right of a hedge. At the bottom the path comes out on to a road. Turn left, then after crossing a bridge the road bends left to reach a road junction. Go left again to keep in the same direction to reach the Bridge Inn pub. Go right at the pub on to a short road which leads to a car park. Go through the car park on to a path which skirts round a pond then stay on this path close to the river for about half a mile until another pond is reached on the left. After passing the pond, go over a stile on the left next to a gate. At the other side fork right to go uphill to enter trees.

Pass to the right of an old stile and carry on uphill to reach a field at the top of the banking. Turn right, and with a hedge on the right cross a total of three fields keeping in the same direction. At the end of the third field, just before the path enters woods, turn left on to a path which leads uphill. With the woods on the right, further up the hill the path bends right and begins to level off. As it heads towards houses in the distance it is joined by a path coming from the right. Stay to the left of the houses to reach Plumbley Lane. Turn left, then at the top of the lane cross a track on to a path which passes two large storage containers and several barns on the left. The path goes through bushes and trees then cuts straight across the middle of a field. At the top of the field go through more bushes to reach another field. Follow the path to the right as it skirts round this field to reach the top right corner.

Keep in the same direction on a path which is enclosed to start with which leads downhill to a bridge over a stream. The path now bends right as it starts to go uphill, crossing a stile to enter a field. With trees to the right, pass through three fields. At the end of the third field, as the path enters scrubland, a hedge can be seen going uphill to the left. Take a path left here which leads into a small wood. The path goes half right through the wood heading towards houses higher up, and soon emerges back into the car park where the walk started.

Look out for…..

Litfield Farm is a 17c Grade 11 listed building which is surrounded by a collection of five cottages which were once part of the estate.

Birley Hay was an early industrial hamlet from the 1500's. Scythes and other tools were forged under tilt hammers driven by waterwheels.

Dog Suitability

For most of the walk dogs can be safely off-lead. There are just a few fields on the way to Plumbley where there might be sheep.

Refreshments

The Swan Inn at Ridgeway is the perfect place to enjoy food and drink.

Walk No 20 : Ecclesfield

4 miles / 2 hours

Introduction

This pleasant round walk sets off from the centre of Ecclesfield and passes through some really nice countryside, as well as some interesting villages and hamlets on the outskirts of the village. Mainly using field paths and farm tracks, the route also includes a little bit of road walking along quiet country lanes. In an area probably not all that familiar with many people, the route goes through the hamlets of Wood Seats, Wood End and Middleton Green, as well as an area of Ecclesfield known as The Wheel. The route also touches on the outskirts of Whitley, Burncross and Grenoside. There is also some history on the route, the highlight of which is the 15/16c St Mary's church in Ecclesfield which can be seen from miles around.

Walking Group in the hamlet of Wood Seats

104

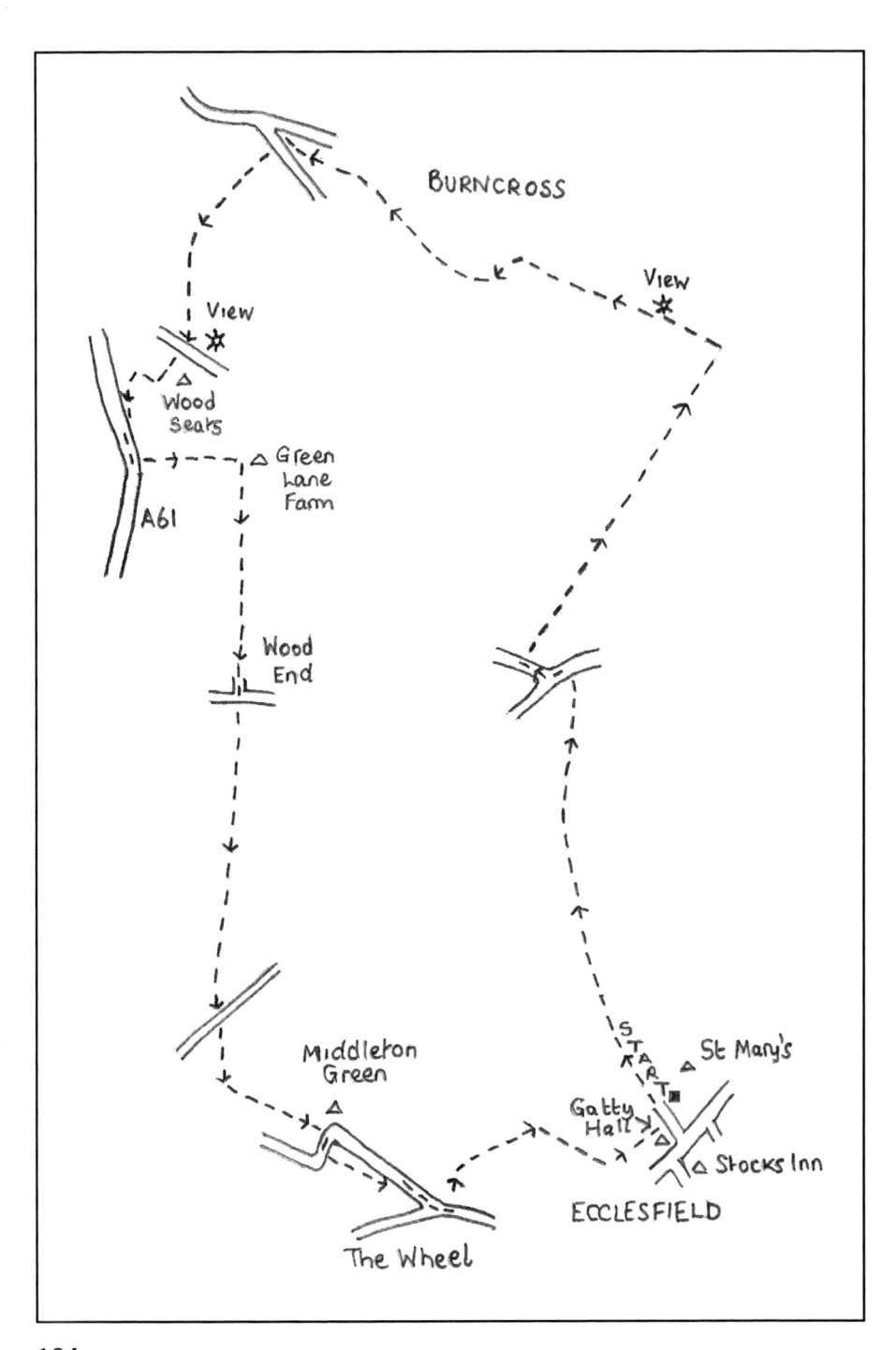

Walk Difficulty

There are a couple of stiff climbs and some tricky stiles to watch out for, and there could also be a lot of mud in winter or after heavy rain, otherwise it's quite an easy walk.

Starting Point

The side entrance to St Mary's Church, Priory Road, Ecclesfield, S35 9XY. What3Words is **stars.large.hammer**

The Route

From the church, go to the end of Priory Road and straight on to a path in front. After a minute or two take a right fork which leads downhill through a field to cross a stream. At the other side the path goes through a long field to reach a driveway to a house. The driveway leads left on to Whitley Lane opposite houses. Go left along the road, then at an immediate junction turn right on to Elliott Lane. After a few yards, take the second path right at the side of houses which leads to a field with a hedge on the right. Stay on this path as it drops down towards trees ahead. Just before the trees are reached, the path goes through a gap in the hedge to carry on downhill to cross a stream. The path now goes slightly left up a steep hill with a hedge to the right. In the top right corner, reach an old track, Windmill Hill Lane.

Go left and stay on the lane for nearly a mile as it becomes a tarmac road further on and reaches Horbury Lane. Take the immediate path left here which says PRIVATE! even though it isn't a private path at all. After a few yards the path enters a narrow wood, and stays to the left of the wood for a few minutes before entering a field. Stay on this obvious path as it climbs to the left of a house to reach Elliott Lane again. Cross slightly right to go into a short field which leads to a private drive at Wood Seats. Go right along the drive, which then bends left to reach a large retaining wall for the A61 above. Go left here to reach the A61 and walk along the main road for about 75 yards to take a farm track on the left. Just before the track reaches a farm take the path right and stay on this path to reach the hamlet of Wood End.

Stay on the road to pass houses on both sides, then at a road ahead, cross over to go over a stile leading into a field. Keeping to the top right of the field the path goes through trees to come out on to Whitley Lane. Cross slightly right into a field and stay to the left of the field to go through the top left corner into another field. Stay to the left again as the path bends slightly left to drop down towards houses on the left at the end of this field. The path leaves the field at Cinder Hill Lane in the hamlet of Middleton Green.

Turn right to walk along Cinder Hill Lane and after passing houses, at a right bend take a path left into a field. Ignore a path right and stay at the bottom of the field as the path bends left through woods to reach Cinder Hill Lane again. Turn right to head towards Ecclesfield passing the cricket club on the left, then just after the road reaches The Wheel take a narrow gennel between houses on the left. Into a field go half right towards a marker post. Through a stile a path goes half left up a short banking. At the top take a little-used grass path right which leads into a horse field. Stay to the left of the field to a stile in the corner and a path which leads back to the church.

Look out for…..

Ecclesfield Church. There has been a church on the site since 7c. The current St Mary's church took 22 years to build and was completed in 1500.

Gatty Hall. The Gatty Memorial Hall was built as a memorial to the Reverend Dr Alfred Gatty, who was vicar of St Mary's from 1839 to 1903. The building was paid for by public subscription and cost £1,300 to build.

Green Lane Farm has an 1825 Grade ll listed cart shed.

Dog Suitability

This is a good walk for dogs as there are plenty of paths and tracks used where there aren't normally any farm animals.

Refreshments

Close to the start of the walk there is The Stocks pub and Le Petit cafe

Walk No 21 : Edale

7.25 miles / 4 hours

Introduction

This is quite a demanding walk with many challenges, but at the same time has all round views throughout its entirety. From Windy Ridge, where the walk begins, the route walk immediately starts with a climb up to Mam Tor and is then followed by a tricky downhill section from Hollins Cross to the Vale of Edale, on the way into Edale village. Following some easy-going field paths to Barber Booth, there's then a 1.5 mile climb up Chapel Gate to get to the top of Rushup Edge to enjoy the fantastic views from up there. The walk from the start of Rushup Edge then just gets better as it goes along, and very soon as Lord's Seat is reached the views on either side are something really special.

The Vale Of Edale

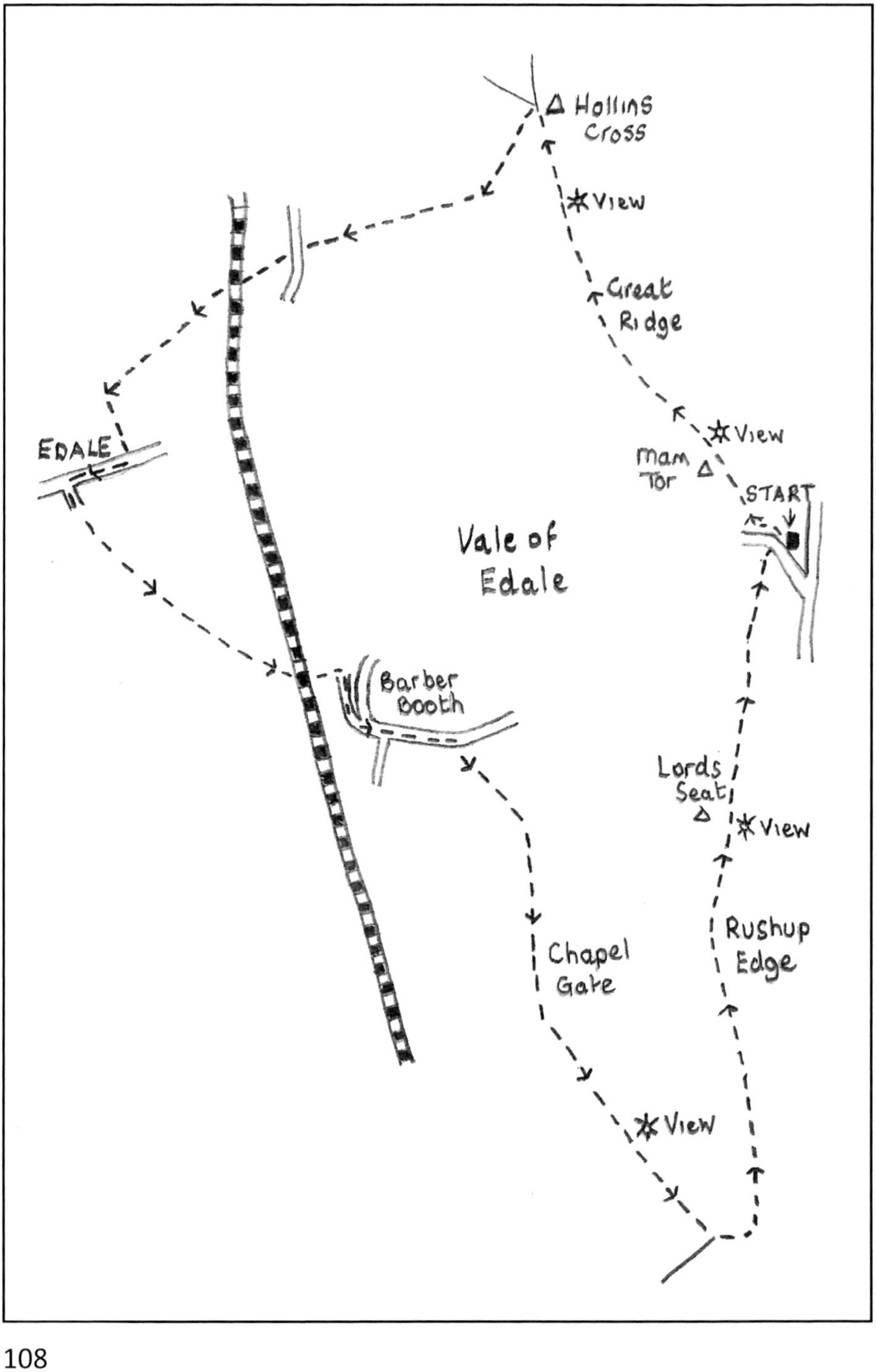

Hollins Cross
View
Great Ridge
View
Mam Tor
START
EDALE
Vale of Edale
Barber Booth
Lords Seat
View
Chapel Gate
Rushup Edge
View

Walk Difficulty

There are two challenging climbs on this walk; the first to get to the top of Mam Tor is short and sharp, whilst the other one up Chapel Gate is a long drag which will take 30-45 minutes. Care needs to be taken on the path down from Hollins Cross, and at Rushup Edge where the going is quite rocky. There could also be the usual mud and standing water throughout the walk.

Starting Point

Mam Nick car park, Castleton S33 8WA. What3words: **mainly.today.opera**

The Route

At the car park find a path at the top which leads into trees, soon bending right as it stays close to the road as it carries on climbing up the hill. Out of the trees the path carries on towards a gate on the right which leads on to a signposted path to Mam Tor. At the top of the hill, pass the trig point to take the path across The Ridge, with it's amazing views on both sides. After passing through 2 gates, after a mile the path reaches a junction of paths with a signpost on the left and an obelisk in the middle of the path. Through a gate on the left, turn sharp left on to a rocky path heading downhill. After a minute or two fork right to carry on downhill in the direction of a farm. Approaching the farm head for a gate about 50 yards to the left of it.

The path soon joins a track leading from the house and heads towards Edale Road. Just before reaching the road take a short path on the left to reach the road directly opposite a path on the other side of the road. Cross the road into an enclosed path, which leads into a field at the top on the left. Walk on the grassed section to the left of the field, then at the corner turn right to go up the side of the field to go under a railway bridge. At the end of the next field go through a stile on the left just before a gate, then go half left through another field, passing to the right of a barn. In the next field keep in the same direction as the path heads towards trees. In the top left corner go through a stile and turn left to enter trees. After crossing a stream carry on to the road, then turn right on to the road into Edale.

In the village centre, with the Nags Head in front, take a track left along the side of a café. After passing a campsite, go down a banking on the left to go through a stile into a field. The path here goes half right and follows a series of marker posts and gates through a number of fields as it stays in roughly the same direction heading towards the railway line. Ignore a signposted path left for Edale station to keep in the same direction until three short fields later the path joins a track from the right which leads to a bridge over the railway. At the other side, the track bends right to reach the hamlet of Barber Booth at a minor road. Turn right to pass a red brick house and stay on this road as it bends left to soon reach a wider road. Keep in the same direction on this road as it crosses a river, and then passes a road leading off to the right. After a quarter of a mile, just before the road starts to bend left, go through a gate on the right on to a track called Chapel Gate.

Chapel Gate winds its way uphill for a mile and a half almost to the top of Rushup Edge, being joined as it rises by several minor paths joining it from the right. At the top though it reaches a path 'T' junction. Leave Chapel Gate here by turning left on to a path on to Rushup Edge. Stay on this path as it passes its highpoint of Lord's Seat on the left, at 550 metres above sea level. Further on, approaching the road take a path which goes slight right and drops down towards trees, cutting the corner of the road off. Cross the road to find the path again which leads back to the car park.

Look out for…..

The Views. This walk is all about the views. From Mam Tor, the Great Ridge and Rushup Edge the landscape all around is amazing. But walking through the Vale Of Edale and looking up at the hills all around is also a great way of enjoying this beautiful part of the Peak District.

Dog Suitability

Dogs well need to be kept under close control for most of the walk due to the possibility of there being sheep in most parts of the walk.

Refreshments

The walk passes The Old Nags Head and Newfold Café in Eyam.

Walk No 22: Totley Moor

5.25 miles / 2.5 hours

Introduction

For anyone who likes moorland walks this is the perfect moorland walk, as apart from a section through the Longshaw Estate the walk takes place entirely on open moorland. Enjoying extensive views all through the walk and using mainly ancient packhorse routes, the paths are fairly decent throughout, making it a fairly easy walk as far as Peak District walks go. Although the village of Totley is entirely within the Sheffield border, the whole of this walk takes place in Derbyshire, and is also entirely within the Peak District. Wildlife lovers may be keen to know that herds of deer can often be seen in this area, as can curlews, skylarks and grouse.

Looking across the Longshaw Estate towards Hope Valley and Kinder Scout

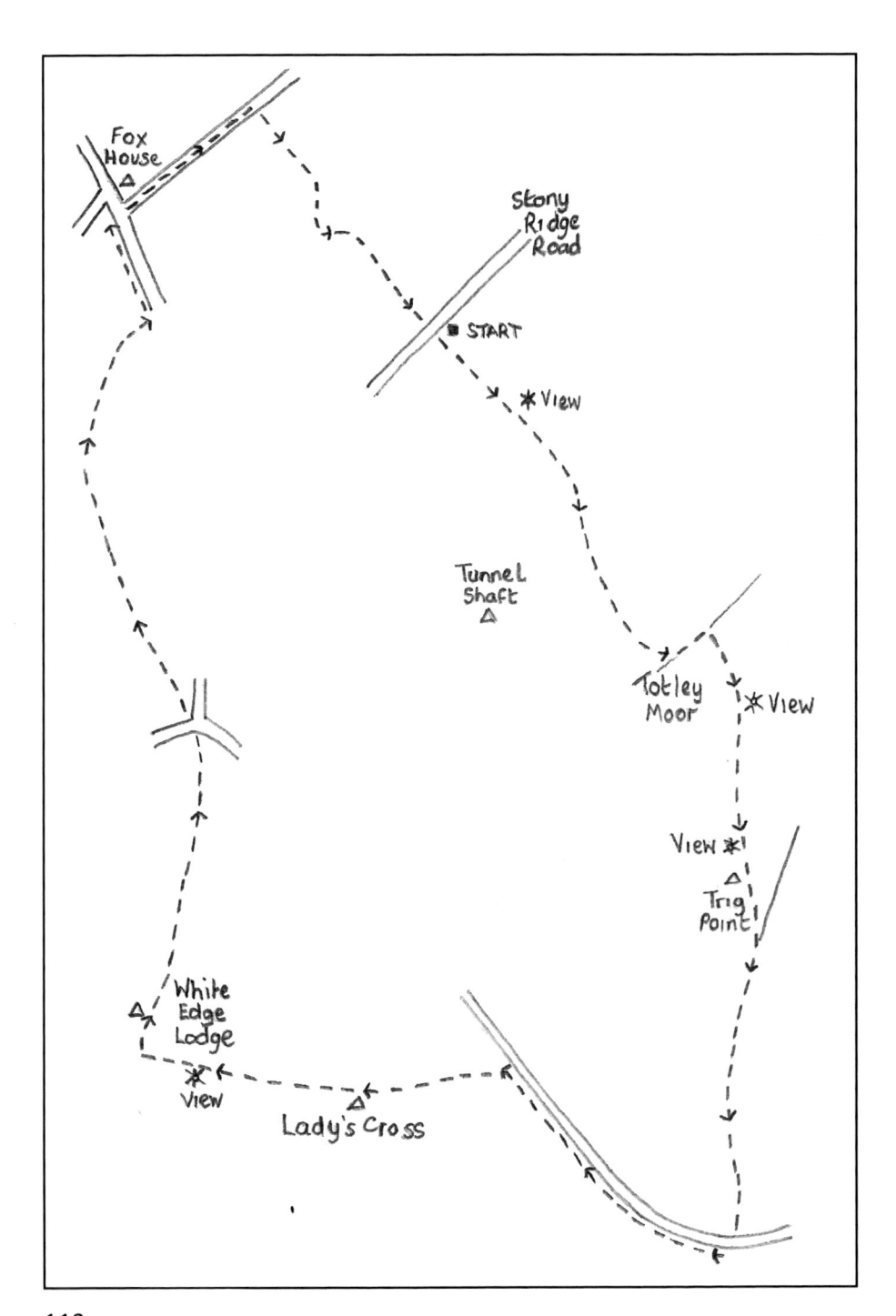

Walk Difficulty

Some of the paths can be muddy in winter and after rain, and there is a boggy section where there is mud all year round, but there are no great climbs or stiles.

Starting Point

A roadside parking area on Stony Ridge Road which approaching the Fox House from Sheffield on Hathersage Road is the left turn which leads to Froggatt and Calver. There is plenty of space to park about 1/3 of a mile along Stony Ridge Road where there are footpath signs on both sides of the road. There is no postcode for the parking area, but What3words are **mock.gently.curl**

The Route

From the car parking area, go through a gate on that side of the road on to a well-used path. Fairly soon, there are extensive views of Sheffield city centre to enjoy on the left, and a ventilation shaft from the Totley to Grindleford railway tunnel on the hillside on the right. After three quarters of a mile, at wooden fencing on the left, Moss Road an old packhorse route joins from the right. Keep in the same direction for 300 yards and just as the path levels out, take an unsigned grassy path right on to Totley Moor.

The path soon climbs steadily uphill in the direction of a trig point on the right. The trig point is 395 metres/1296 feet above sea level, and to appreciate 360-degree views from it, leave the path to visit the trig point, then leave the trig point to the left to re-join the track. Turn right at the track to carry on in the same direction, until after a few minutes the track is joined by a wide grass path coming from the left. Once again, go straight forward as the path reaches a main road after just over half a mile. Cross the road slightly left to go through a gate then turn right on to a path which stays close to the road for three quarters of a mile. The path ends at a gate and a footpath sign on the right. Go left here, taking the right path of two options to gently climb through heather and moorland.

After a quarter of a mile leave the path to look at the Lady's Cross landmark on the left, then return to the path to carry on uphill. Go through the gate at the top, then take the path which veers to the right to head towards a house, White Edge Lodge. Keep to the right of the house and walk along the drive away from the house until it reaches the road. Cross over the island between roads and head for the white gate ahead. Through the gate walk along the grassy path for just under half a mile to reach a gate which enters woodland. Go to the right of the gate here, on to another grassy path which stays to the right of trees until it ends at a small gate on the left.

Go through the gate and into the trees and stay on this path, passing a car park left, then crossing the road which leads into the car park to enter more trees. Carry on in the same direction, staying as close to the road on the right as possible to come out on to the road opposite the Fox House pub. Cross the road to the pub, then go round the corner of the pub to walk up the main road, passing the pub car park and parked cars. After 350 yards cross the road to a signposted path leading on to moorland. Stay on this path as it winds its way back to Stony Ridge Road.

Look out for…..

Totley Tunnel Ventilation Shaft is 6 feet tall and 15 feet across and was built in the 1890's. The tunnel is over 600 feet below and if there is what looks like smoke coming out of the shaft it is in fact a type of condensation. Totley Moss, the area above the tunnel is very wet and that water seeps down and drips into the tunnel making the atmosphere down there very damp. As trains pass through, they push air along the tunnel and combined with the temperature differentials between the tunnel and the outside air, this causes damp air to rise up the shaft and appear as mist.

Lady's Cross is believed to have been a wayside marker for ancient packhorse trails across the moor, but it also served as a marker at the junction of the boundaries between Hathersage, Holmesfield and Totley. The top of the cross has been broken off, and it was first mentioned in a document of 1263. To the superstitious, god-fearing medieval traveller, these bleak and desolate moors were the haunt of boggarts and other malevolent creatures. The sight of a cross would have been a comforting one, and offered them some protection from the demons that inhabited the moor.

White Edge Lodge was originally a gamekeeper's cottage on the Duke of Rutland's Longshaw Estate but nowadays is owned by the National Trust and rented out as a holiday cottage. Many of its original features have been retained, such as the wooden beams and exposed brick walls, and the water supply is still fed from a nearby spring. Its spectacular location led to it being featured as Moor House in the 2011 adaptation of Charlotte Brontë's classic novel "Jane Eyre".

Fox House was built in 1773 and is one of the highest pubs in Yorkshire at 1,132 foot above sea level. It was famous as a calling place for carrier carts and stagecoaches in the past, but equally so for illegally serving wagon drivers during "the small hours". Originally called "The Travellers Rest" it was later named after the Fox Family of Callow near Hathersage. A story goes that one snowy night at closing time, a Stoney Middleton man set off home from the inn a little less than sober. The next day he was found in a garden nearby, covered in snow but miraculously still alive. He was thawed out and given a meal and then went home without any ill effects from his night in the snow.

Dog Suitability

Throughout the walk there could be the possibility of sheep close by, so dogs will need to be kept under close control

Refreshments

The Fox House pub and the café at Longshaw are both excellent places to use for food and drink.

WHEN IT COMES TO FINE ALES ...
FARMERS BLONDE
YORKSHIRE FARMER
FARMERS BROWN COW
FARMERS STOUT
FARMERS PALE ALE
... you'll find us outstanding in our field
BRADFIELD BREWERY
BRADFIELD BREWERY SHEFFIELD
TRY A TASTE of TRADITION
On-Site Brewery Shop open: Monday to Friday 8am - 4pm & Saturdays 10am-4pm.
info@bradfieldbrewery.com • 0114 2851118
www.bradfieldbrewery.com
Bradfield Brewery Limited, Watt House Farm, High Bradfield, Sheffield, S6 6LG
Visit our page on Facebook or follow us on Twitter for the latest news and offers.

Walk No 23 : Baslow

7.5 miles / 4 hours

Introduction

The nice thing about this walk is that from the very start there is something of interest to see, and this carries on throughout the walk. From the starting point there is a pleasant climb through the streets of Baslow up to Baslow Edge for the views up there and a look at Wellington's Monument. Then it's a steady stroll across to Birchin Edge and Nelson's Monument before the route heads off to the Robin Hood area to finish the walk off through the Chatsworth estate. Some nice paths through woodland, and along the top of a couple of edges lead to the Hunting Tower, and after passing the remains of the aqueduct, Chatsworth House is passed on the way back to the start. Old packhorse routes, moorland tracks and estate paths are all used on this walk which manages to fit so much in from start to finish.

Summer heather in bloom on the way up to Baslow Edge

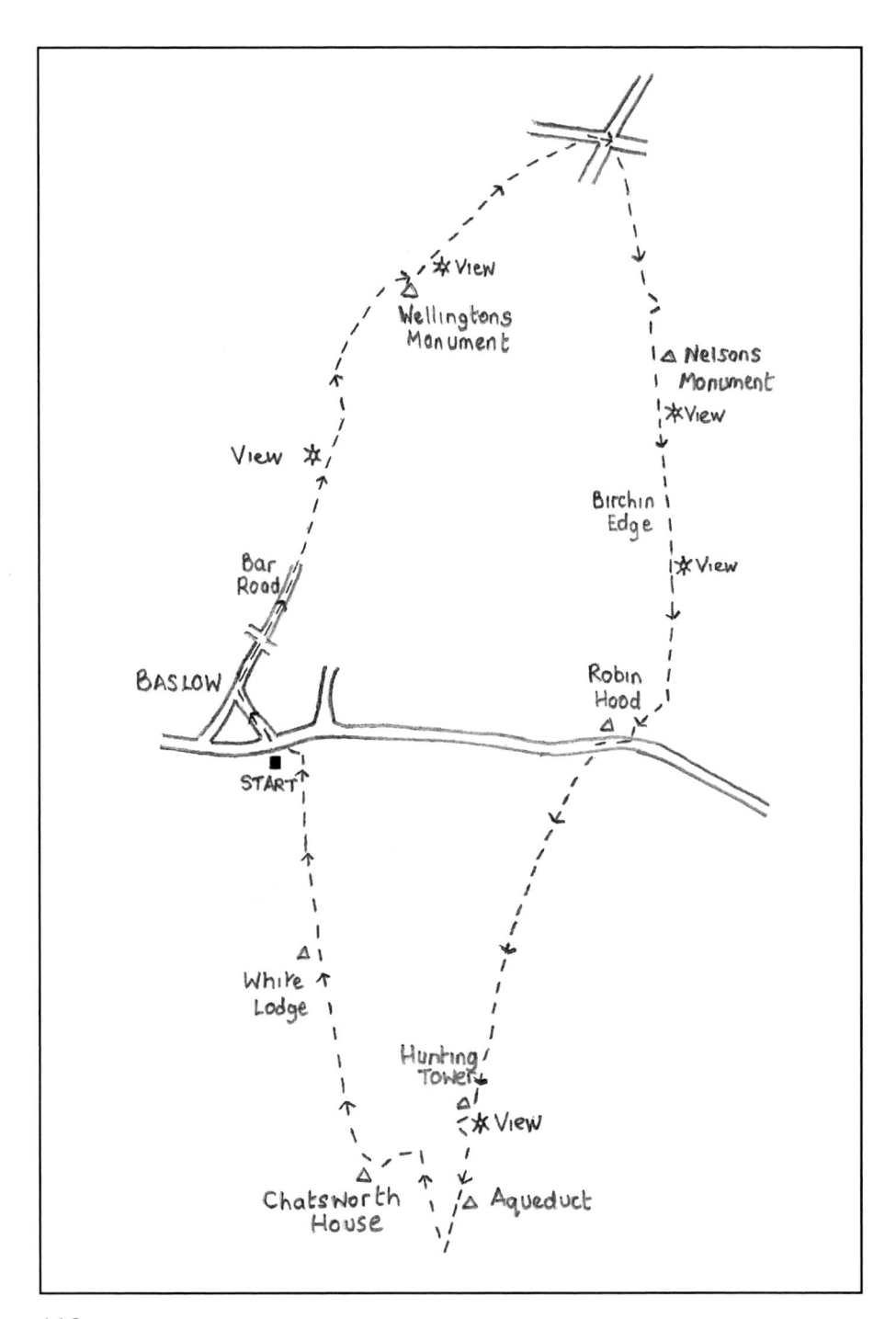

Walk Difficulty

There's a fairly long climb at the start, a short sharp climb on to Birchin Edge, a slightly tricky descent off Birchin Edge, and a section alongside a steep drop to watch out for. There are also a couple of boggy sections to negotiate too.

Starting Point

Nether End Car Park, Church Ln, Baslow, DE45 1S. There is also free on-street parking locally. What3words: **models.goggle.jugs**

The Route

From the car park cross the main road to walk up Eaton Hill. At the grass triangle bear right on to Bar Road to start the climb up to Baslow Edge. Up the hill, where the houses end, the road becomes a track but is still known as Bar Road. Through a gate, the track bends twice until after almost a mile it reaches the top at a point where a major path leads left towards a rocky outcrop. Bear right here to stay on Bar Road, passing Wellingtons Monument on the right. After almost a mile the track reaches Clodhall Lane.

Turn right to walk down the road to crossroads. Cross over to go through a gate on the right, then take a left fork, ignoring a minor path going left further on, to remain on the main path as it passes through boggy ground. The path climbs steadily towards the rockface of Birchin Edge ahead in the distance and after half a mile it reaches a large rock on the right. Almost opposite take a narrow path which leads to the rockface, and then climbs up to the top of Birchin Edge. At the trig point turn right to follow close to the edge passing Nelson's monument, and just behind it 'The Three Ships'.

After five minutes or so the path bends right, and drops down steeply through a tricky section of rocks to return to the path left earlier to climb up on to the edge. Turn left here and stay on this path as it leads to the road. Turn right, passing the Robin Hood pub as the road joins the main road to carry on in the same direction. After just over 100 yards, cross the road to take a path which leads down some steps to cross a stream. After going up steps at the other side the path reaches a track going left and right. Go straight across on to a path signed for Beeley and the Swiss Lake.

After going over a ladder stile the path goes to the left to follow a fence to start with, and then a wall with sheer drops on the right. After going over a stile go through a squeeze stile right to descend steps. At the bottom the path goes left and continues with a wall first to the right and then to the left. Another stile leads into a field where the path stays to the edge to reach a wall stile. Over the stile, the path goes uphill to the left to follow a wall and then go over another ladder stile.

At the other side the path turns left and stays next to a wall to reach a stony track. Go right along the track as it becomes tarmacked and reaches a crossroads. Go straight across to the Hunting Tower to enjoy the views from there. Below the Hunting Tower is an estate road. Drop down on to it and turn left and walk along it as it heads gently downhill, and after five minutes or so reaches the ruined aqueduct on the left. Carry on in the same direction to soon reach another estate road crossing left and right. Go right, and stay on this road as it carries on downhill, bending to the left at the bottom to reach Chatsworth House car park. The stable block is worth a visit to the left, and from there it's just a case of choosing which way to get back to Baslow.

The quickest way is to cut through the car park towards the grass, and then to walk diagonally across the grass to head towards the bottom path where the cricket pitch is. Once on this path, keep in the same direction as it passes the White Lodge and eventually passes through a kissing gate and joins a lane. At the end of the lane a road is reached to turn left on to, to return to the car park.

Look out for…..

Wellingtons Monument which is dedicated to the Duke of Wellington and celebrates his victory at Waterloo in 1815. It was erected by a local, Dr Wrench, who felt the need to counterbalance the memorial dedicated to Admiral Nelson on Birchen Edge. Wrench served as an army surgeon in the Crimean War and later in India at the time of the Indian Mutiny. After retiring from the army, he settled in Baslow where for the next 50 years he served as a physician to the Chatsworth estate, and to the people of Baslow.

Nelsons Monument. Derbyshire had its Nelson's Column only five years after Trafalgar, while Londoners had to wait a further thirty for theirs! It was erected in 1810 by John Brightman, a local businessman from Baslow and was restored in 1992 by the 1805 Club which was formed in 1990 to assist in the preservation of monuments and memorials relating to Nelson and other seafarers of the Georgian era. Three nearby outcrops called the "Ship Rocks" have been carved with the names of three of Nelson's ships: Victory, Defiance and Royal Soverin.

The Hunting Tower was built in the 1570s and was sited on the crest of the hill to provide extensive views of the deer park, both for locating deer, observing the hunting, and as a place for holding banquets.

The Aqueduct dates from 1839 at the time when Joseph Paxton designed the pools and fountains at Chatsworth for the 6th Duke of Devonshire. It formed part of the flow of water that supplied the Cascade in the Chatsworth gardens. It is believed to have been inspired by a similar but much larger structure in a grand garden near Kassel in Germany.

Dog Suitability

On top of Baslow Edge and in the Birchin Edge there could be sheep and cows, but for the rest of the walk, dogs can be off-lead.

Refreshments

There are numerous pubs and cafes in the centre of Baslow, and during the walk the Robin Hood Inn is passed about half way round, There are various places at Chatsworth House to obtain food and drinks as well.

Walk No 24 : Mayfield Valley

4 miles / 2 hours

Introduction

The Mayfield Valley is so named after the May Brook which runs down the valley from Fulwood Head to the Porter Brook. Situated between Ringinglow and Fulwood, there is a lot of history in this area, much of it connected to both these villages, and on this walk there will be much of it to enjoy. There are old schools, workhouse cottages, a 'Hole in the wall' farm, a 16c Hall and the site of a 17c mill all passed en route, to mention just a few. Mayfield Valley itself is bordered by the Porter Valley on one side which the route also goes through where both valleys roll into each other. As there is no clear route through the Mayfield Valley, this figure-of-eight walk goes through two different parts of the valley using field paths, wooded sections alongside the Porter Brook, and some road walking to link it all together.

Looking down the valley towards Mayfield Mill House

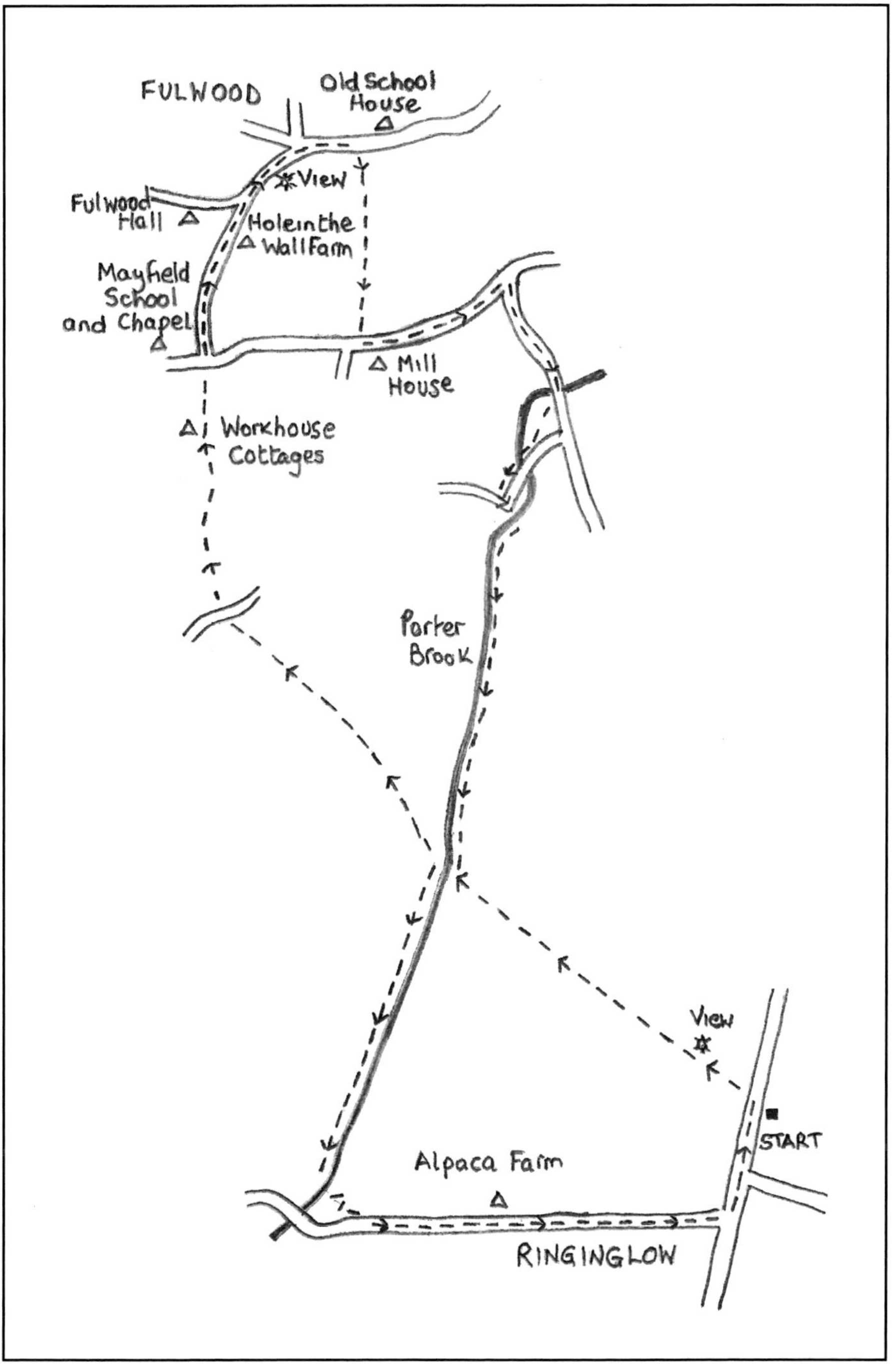

FULWOOD
Old School House
View
Fulwood Hall
Hole in the Wall Farm
Mayfield School and Chapel
Mill House
Workhouse Cottages
Porter Brook
View
START
Alpaca Farm
RINGINGLOW

Walk Difficulty

There is a fairly steep downhill section at the start of the walk where care must be taken, and there will be muddy sections in winter and after rain, but overall this is quite an easy walk.

Starting Point

There is a parking area on the left on Ringinglow Road, just before the junction with Sheephill Road, coming from the Sheffield direction. Postcode S11 7TS. What3Words: **push.pulled.quick**

The Route

From the parking area cross the road and turn right to walk along the road. After about 100 yards take an enclosed path left which passes the back of the Alpaca Farm before going through a gate into a field. Straight ahead the field drops down steeply to reach a stile at the bottom. Over the stile turn left on to a track which immediately bends right to reach a path going left and right. Turn right to go through a squeeze stile then go over a stile immediately to the left to follow a clear path which leads diagonally across a rough field. After passing through a few trees the path continues through two more fields to reach a lane at a farmhouse on the right.

Turn left along the lane for 30 yards then go through a gate on the right to enter a field. Keep to the left side of the field with a wall alongside to reach a gate at the bottom left-hand corner. Through the gate the path veers right to reach houses and a driveway at Workhouse Green. Further on, when the track reaches a lane, either turn left to look at Mayfield Chapel or go straight across on to David Lane. After passing the Hole in the Wall farm bear right at the road junction to walk along School Green Lane, which soon starts to pass houses on the left. At the next road junction keep on School Green Lane as it bends right and starts to go downhill.

After 50 yards there is a signposted path on the right which leads on to a short, enclosed path between a house drive and a farm. Either take this path or walk 50 yards further down School Green Lane to look at the old school on the left, now a private residence. Back on the path back up the lane, over a stile, the path cuts diagonally right through a field towards trees. Through two more stiles the path crosses another field to come out on to Mark Lane.

Straight opposite is the site of Mayfield Mill, an old flour mill, where Mill House an animal sanctuary now stands. Turn left to walk along Mayfield Road. At the end of the road turn right, taking care to walk along this busy road for about 100 yards. After crossing the river take the path right to head up the Porter Valley. After about fifty yards go right at the fork, although the left path leads to a road which goes in the same direction, so either route can be taken. After a few minutes, the path reaches the road at a squeeze stile. Here, go left, and then immediately turn right to take a track which carries on uphill next to the Porter Brook.

With fields to the left, after just over a quarter of a mile, the path passes the hill from earlier in the walk. Carry on past it as the track bends right to reach the same path going left and right as before. Go left this time to carry on up the Porter Valley into a section known as Porter Clough. After about 10 minutes the path reaches a path junction. Go left to cross a bridge on to a path which zigzags its way up the hill and then into a car park. Go through the car park on to the road and walk along the road to the road junction at Ringinglow, passing the Alpaca Farm entrance on the way. Turn left at the junction, and the car parking area is about 100 yards down the road.

Look out for…..

Workhouse Cottages, built in 1740, housed inmates from the Ecclesall Bierlow Workhouse who collected fruit from fields and hedgerows, and grew garden produce to be sent to the Workhouse.

Mayfield School was built in 1875 and ceased being a school in 1944. Later it was turned into an Environmental Studies centre and children were brought from Sheffield schools to study the delightful countryside and natural habitat. After remaining empty since 2009 the building was converted into private residences in 2020.

Mayfield Wesleyan Reform chapel dates back to 1872 when a Mr J.A. Grange of Mayfield House converted part of one of his barns into a preaching house. It was said that local inhabitants first gathered in a chamber over a cowshed for worship. After Mr Grange's death, the new owners needed the barn for other uses and in 1896 the present chapel was built, with the cost being in the region of £550.

'Hole in the Wall' farm, or David Lane farm to give it its proper name is so called because opposite the farm was a spring used by local people as their source of fresh water. When the land became enclosed under the Enclosures Act, the commissioners stipulated that a hole had to be left in the wall to allow access to the spring. When the Redmires dams were being constructed, many farms in the area, including this one, became ale houses used by the navvies, and they called this farm the Hole in the Wall pub and the name stuck.

Fulwood Hall. A hall existed on the site in the late 15th century, as it was mentioned in deeds from the reign of Henry V11. In 1620 John Fox, a man with considerable possessions in Upper Hallam and the parish of Bradfield, was granted permission to purchase and clear a portion of woodland, and there he built Fulwood Hall. It was the family seat of the Fox family for six or seven generations, and it is said that the last heir wasted his estate. Apparently, 'it was the' drink that did it.'

The Old School House on School Green Lane in Fulwood, Sheffield, England. This Grade II Listed Building dates from 1736. It is now use as a private dwelling.

Mayfield Mill. The first Industrial use of any of Sheffield's rivers occurred in 1641 when Ulysses Fox of Fulwood Hall built a corn mill on the Mayfield Brook where the mill was situated.

Dog Suitability

Apart from the path up the Porter Valley, the rest of the walk is either through fields of sheep or on roads, so it's not a great walks for dogs.

Refreshments

There is a café at the Alpaca Farm and numerous pubs in the area.

Walk No 25 : Dove Dale & Ilam Hall

8 miles / 4.5 hours

Introduction

Dove Dale is one of the iconic places to visit in the White Peak area of the Peak District and a good part of the Dale is walked later in the walk. To start with though, the picturesque village of Ilam is where the walk starts, and after a quick look at Ilam Hall, the route leads down to the River Manifold for some riverside walking before then heading off on the long climb needed to reach Castern Hall. From there it's field paths and farm tracks to get down to Dove Dale via another old hall at Stanshope, followed by a path through the pretty Hope Dale, which is a 'dry' dale. Hope Dale leads into Dove Dale and a lovely walk alongside the River Dove to enjoy before crossing fields next to the Isaac Walton pub to return to the start.

Ilam Hall with Thorpe Cloud in the distance

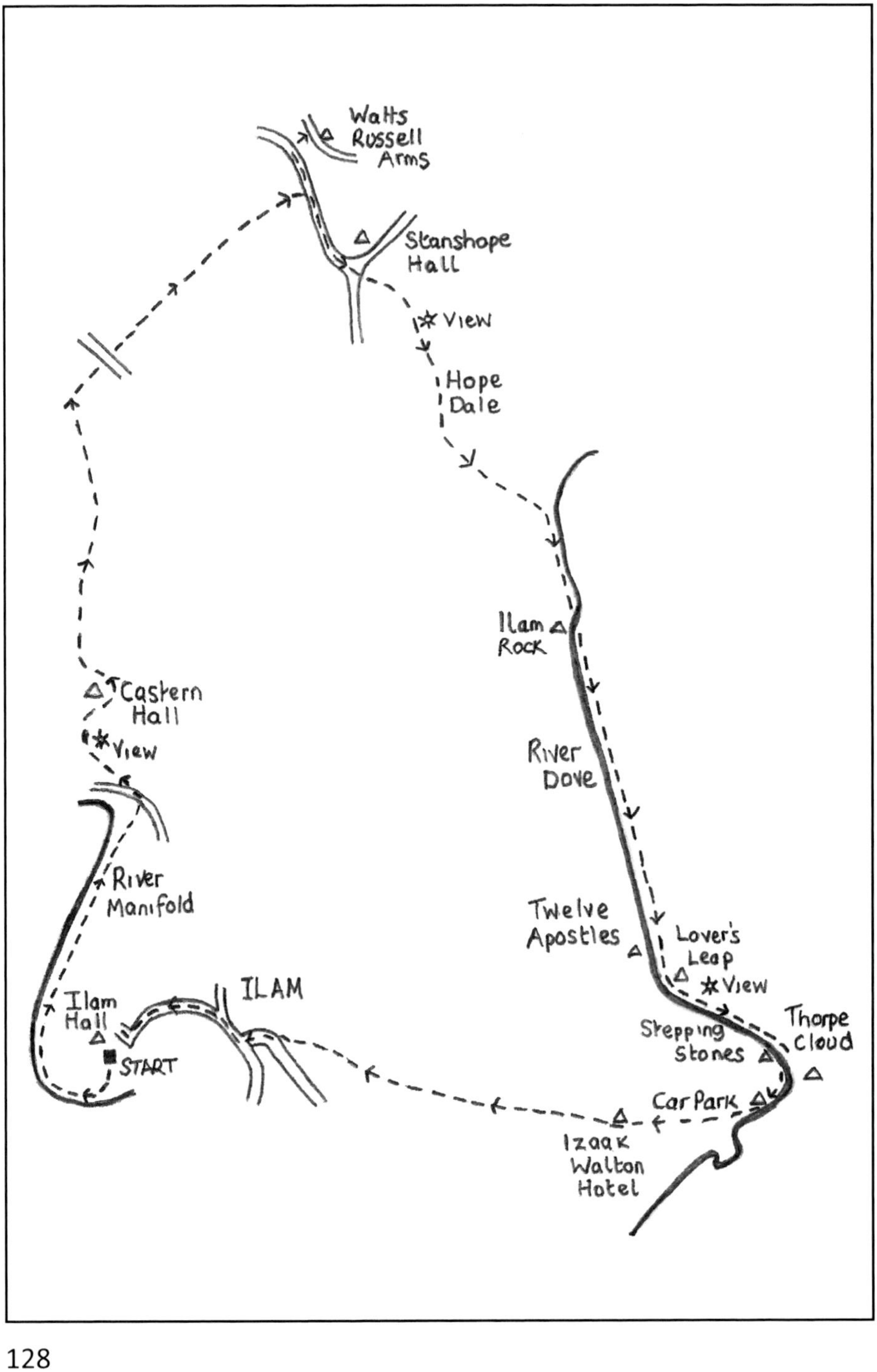
Watts
Russell
Arms
Stanshope
Hall
View
Hope
Dale
Ilam
Rock
River
Dove
Twelve
Apostles
Lover's
Leap
View
Thorpe
Cloud
Stepping
Stones
Car Park
Izaak
Walton
Hotel
ILAM
Ilam
Hall
START
River
Manifold
View
Castern
Hall

Walk Difficulty

Although there is a long climb early in the walk, this is a fairly easy route apart from there being a lot of stiles to cross.

Starting Point

Ilam Hall car park, Ilam, DE6 2AZ. What3words: **sway.lake.beeline**

The Route

From the car park go to the front of the Hall to go down steps to the formal gardens. Here, turn right and leave the gardens through an exit at the end of the path. Turn right here to go down steps towards the River Manifold. At the bottom of the steps turn right and stay on this path which stays close to the river for just under a mile until it emerges on to a road. Go left and then after about 100 yards take a drive right which leads uphill to Castern Hall. Round the back of the Hall the drive becomes a track and crosses a cattle grid. Immediately after this, as the track bends right, take a path left.

After crossing a stile next to a gate, stay on a wide grassy track with a wall left to cross 2 fields, then just after entering the third field the track bears right and leaves the wall to cut across a banking. Further up the field go through the right-hand gate of two, and then in the next field the path goes half left to a gate, passing a mound on the left on the way. Through the gate after a few yards take a grass track right with a wall on the left and old spoil heaps on the right. Ahead, in the distance, can be seen a tall signpost. Head for this and pass through a squeeze stile next to it which leads on to a lane. Cross the lane to go through another squeeze stile leading into the next field. Go half left across this field as indicated by the 'Public Footpath to Hopedale' sign to the next squeeze stile which is situated in a wall.

Through this stile keep straight on, crossing four fields with a wall on the left. In the fifth field the path leaves the wall to head to the top right corner to reach another stile. Through two more fields the path reaches Stanshope Lane. At this point, if required, a short diversion can be made to The Watts Russell Arms by turning left and walking along the road for about 350 yards before taking a path right which after a couple of minutes leads to the pub.

Back at the point where Stanshope Lane was reached, turn right and walk along the road to shortly reach Stanshope Hall. After passing the Hall the road bends right. At this point cross the road to take a track left. 80 yards down the track take a path right signposted Dovedale via Hopedale. The route here heads towards Hopedale, a deep ravine which can be seen up ahead. The path crosses several fields and stiles whilst keeping in the same direction as it heads down to the dale. Once in the dale the path keeps going downhill to reach the River Dove and Dove Dale about a mile after leaving Stanshope. Turn right to follow the Dove for a short while, and with Ilam Rock on the right, cross a bridge to reach the other side of the river.

Turn right here to walk through Dove Dale until after about a mile and a half stepping stones across the river are reached. Either cross the stepping stones, or go straight forward to cross a bridge on the right further on. In both cases a lane at the other side of the river is used to reach the Dove Dale car parks, where the one to the left has a refreshment stand and toilets. The route continues though by walking through the overflow car park on the right. Half way along the car park take a path on the right which leads into a field. The path soon passes to the right of the Izaac Walton Hotel and stays in the same direction, going through two more fields before reaching a road on the outskirts of Ilam village. Turn right to enter the village, and then at the junction turn right again to walk towards Ilam Hall. After a few yards go left on to the hall driveway to return to the car park.

Look out for…..

Ilam Hall. The first Ilam Hall was built by the Port family in the 16th century but this was demolished by Jesse Watts Russell to make way for his much grander hall of the 1820s. Most of the hall was demolished in the 1920s before Sir Robert McDougall bought the estate and donated it to the National Trust in 1934. Since then, the main remaining part of the hall has been used as a Youth Hostel and the grounds have been open to the public.

River Manifold is 12 miles long and rises at Flash Head south of Buxton and joins the River Dove just beyond Ilam. For part of its course the Manifold runs underground, and from May to October the river is often completely dry.

Castern Hall has been owned by the Hurt family since 16c. It is thought that there has always been a dwelling at Castern since the earliest of days. The fields around are littered with Iron Age, Bronze Age and even Stone Age remains. There are Roman remains in the cellars and there have been important Roman and Saxon finds around the house. The grange at Castern was owned by Burton Abbey until the Dissolution of the Monasteries when it was acquired by Roger Hurt, who settled there in the mid-16th Century.

Stanshope Hall has been part of the Stanshope Estate since the 1500's. The current house is Grade II listed and was built in the 1700's. It is currently a hotel and is described on websites as follows: "An elegant country house, Stanshope Hall features cosy log fires, home-cooked food, and pretty gardens in the heart of the Peak District"

Dove Dale highlights are many, but here are just a few to look out for: Ilam Rock, Lover's Leap, The Twelve Apostles rock formation, Thorpe Cloud, the stepping stones.

Izaak Walton Hotel is so-named because of the 17c author Izaak Walton who wrote a famous fishing book 'The Compleat Angler' in 1653, after spending time fishing on the River Dove, 200 yards from the pub.

Dog Suitability

Along the River Manifold dogs can be off-lead, but after that there are fields where there could be sheep, also although there aren't usually sheep on the path through Dove Dale, they can often be seen higher up the slopes.

Refreshments

Half way through the walk a small diversion could be made to the Watts Russell Arms at Hopedale, and there is also a shop at Ilam Hall, a kiosk at Dove Dale car park, and the Isaac Walton pub near the end of the walk.

Walk No 26 : Hallam Moors

5 miles / 2.5 hours

Introduction

This is another walk which is both in the Peak District, and also within the Sheffield city boundary. It takes place on high ground up at Redmires in an area between Redmires reservoirs and the Rivelin Valley known as Hallam Moors. Starting with great views across the moors towards Rivelin and Rod Moor, the route then heads off through a lovely area known as Reddicar Clough to reach Wyming Brook Drive, a disused road. Following a steady woodland climb, the Redmires Reservoir Cottages are reached at the top of Wyming Brook, before the walk finishes with a circuit of the three reservoirs to return to the start.

Looking over Hallam Moors towards Rod Moor

Headstone △

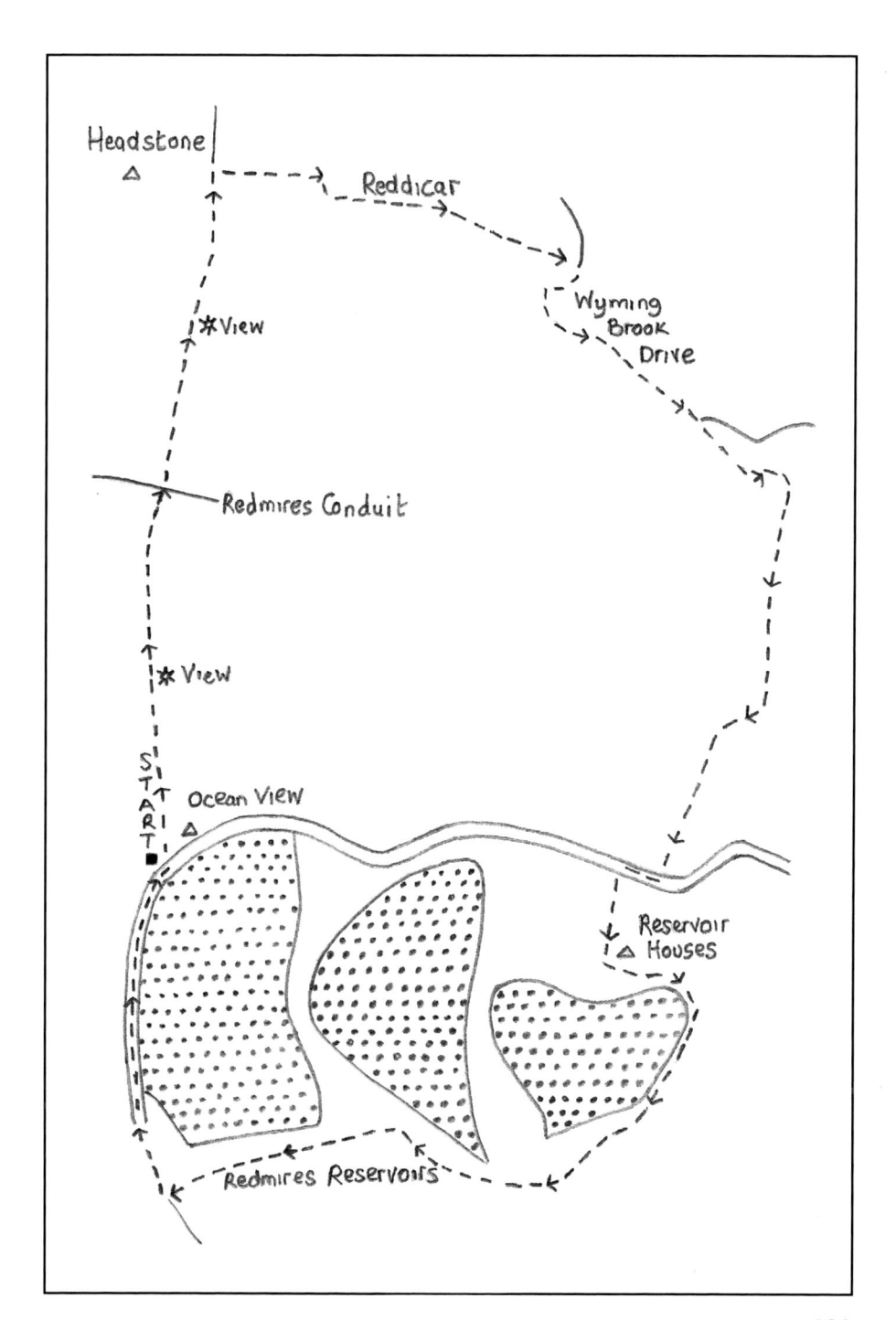

Reddicar

Wyming Brook Drive

*View

Redmires Conduit

*View

START

Ocean View △

Reservoir Houses △

Redmires Reservoirs

Walk Difficulty

This is a fairly easy walk on mainly good paths, with just a short section across Hallam Moors at the start which can be wet and boggy, as can a couple of small sections of the reservoir path.

Starting Point

Upper Redmires Reservoir car park, Redmires Road, Sheffield S10 4QZ. What3words are **trucks.pace.rises**.

The Route

Facing the reservoir, leave the car park through a gate on the left. Turn left on to a path which leads uphill on to Hallam Moors. Keep on this path heading in roughly the same direction until after about 15 minutes it reaches Redmires Conduit. Cross over the conduit path to go over a stile to still carry on in the same direction on a path which now leads downhill. After about a quarter of a mile the path reaches cross paths, with the Headstone rock formation to the left. Go right here on a feint path through heather which after a few minutes reaches a gate. Through the gate turn right to walk alongside a fence to soon reach another gate on the right.

Turn left, away from the gate, to head down through Reddicar Hollow to reach Wyming Brook Drive at the bottom of the hill. Turn right to walk along this old road, then after just under half a mile at a fork go right to climb up to the top of Wyming Brook Nature Reserve. Pass through the car park at the top to come out on to Redmires Road. Turn right to walk up the road for a short while before turning left on to a service road for the ex-water authority houses. After passing between the houses, go past a drive on the left, to take a path just after it which leads uphill through trees.

Coming out of the trees, the path bends right to reach a path left heading towards the road, with the Lower Redmires Reservoir on the right. Ignore this path to carry on straight forward to reach a stile in front, and a gate to the right. Go through the gate to walk next to the lower reservoir. After a short while the path climbs to reach the dam wall for the second reservoir. Stay on the path as it leaves this reservoir further on to cut through marshland.

After the path reaches the dam wall for the upper reservoir it starts to bend left and climb to go through bushes to reach a cross path opposite a stile. Turn right to cross a small bridge, and stay on this path as it bends right to reach Redmires Road. Walk along the road to return to the car park.

Look out for…..

Ocean View public house which was situated on the site of the car park. It was opened in 1830 and closed in 1885. Whilst the reservoirs were being built it was frequented by the navvies who lived in tents and temporary homes nearby. After the reservoir building was complete, the pub struggled to attract business, and closed within a few years.

Redmires Conduit was built in the 1830s to supply water to Sheffield. It taps the source of the river Rivelin out on the moor, and bends round the side of the hill and continues down to the Crookes area of Sheffield.

Wyming Brook Drive was built during the depression of the 1920's to provide employment for out-of-work navvies as the interest in driving for pleasure was increasing in the country.

Redmires Reservoirs are fed from various small streams including Fairthorn Clough from the Hallam Moors. The three reservoirs were built to supply clean drinking water to Sheffield following the Cholera epidemic in 1832. The old water treatment works located beside the lower reservoir dates back to 1950, and supplied water to the south-western outer areas of Sheffield utilising the Ringinglow and Rud Hill service reservoirs.

Dog Suitability

For a lot of the walk dogs can be off lead, there is just the section across Hallam Moors where they will need to be led as there is sheep there for most of the year.

Refreshments

There are three pubs in Lodge Moor for refreshments; the Three Merry Lads, The Sportsman and The Shiny Sheff.

Walk No 27 : Bolsterstone

8.25 miles / 4 hours

Introduction

Mostly in the Peak District, and totally within Sheffield, this walk takes place in a beautiful part of the city which is nowhere near as busy as more popular places nearby. Featuring More Hall and Broomhead Reservoirs at the start and end of the walk, the route also includes a look at Bolsterstone village, and an interesting section from Bolsterstone on to Whitwell Moor which has great views to Stocksbridge and the Don Valley on one side, and the Ewden Valley on the other. After a steep climb at the start to get up to Bolsterstone this is an easy walk on mainly good paths. This walk is all about views though. From up above looking down, and from down below looking up!

White Lee Moor and Broomhead Reservoir looking down from Bolsterstone

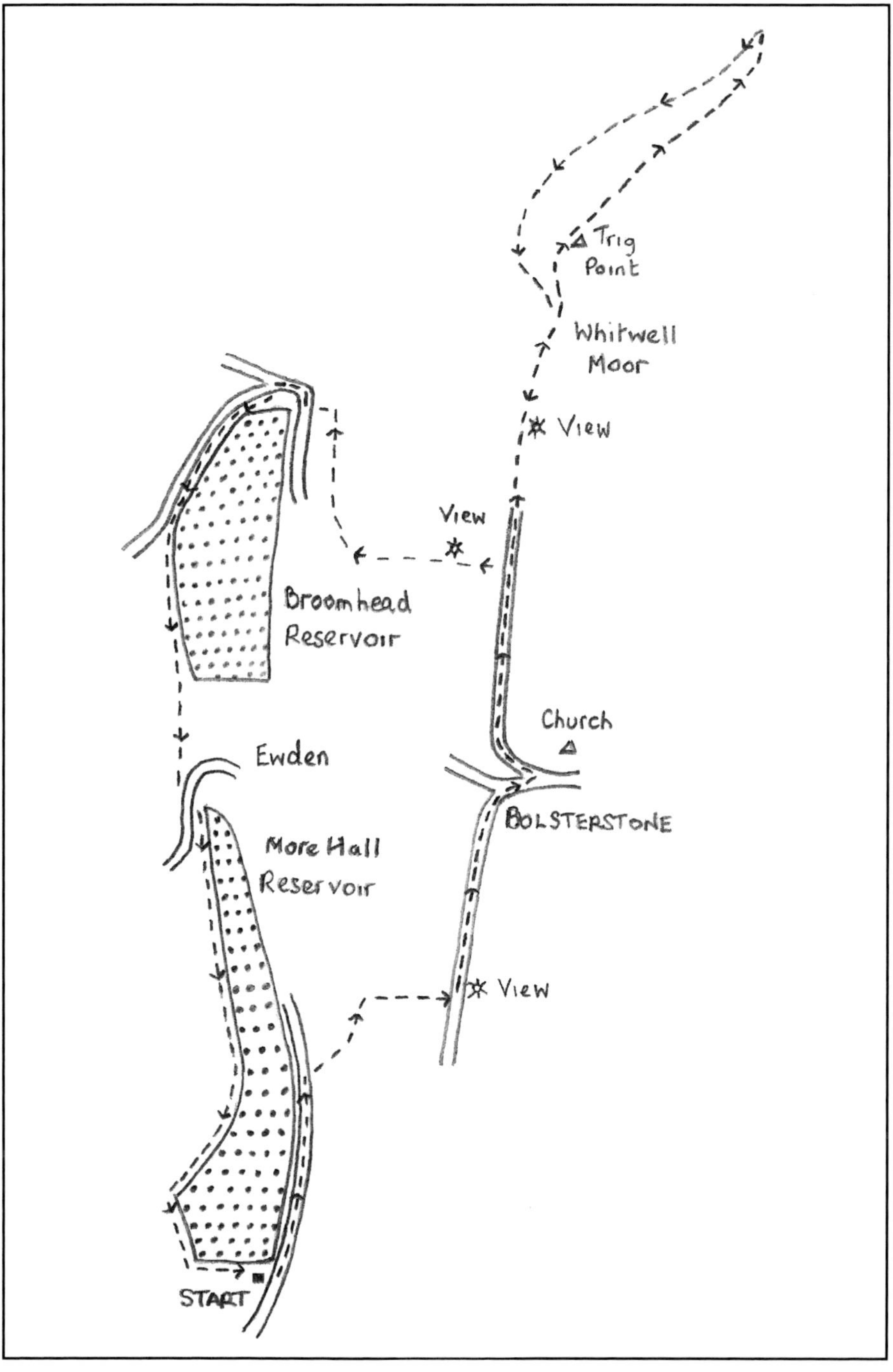

Trig Point
Whitwell Moor
View
View
Broomhead Reservoir
Church
Ewden
BOLSTERSTONE
More Hall Reservoir
View
START

Walk Difficulty

The path leading up from More Hall to Bolsterstone is pretty steep but is only half a mile in total, so should only take about ten minutes or so. There are quite a few stiles too, some tricky, and apart from that, there are just a couple of muddy sections to watch out for.

Starting Point

More Hall Reservoir dam wall situated on the reservoir service road, found next to More Hall Lane at Wharncliffe Side on Manchester Road, A6012. No postcode for the dam wall, but What3Words are **jolt.pace.prepare**

The Route

From More Hall Reservoir dam wall, walk along the road in the direction of Ewden Village. After about ten minutes at a 20mph sign take a signed footpath right. Over the stile the path goes uphill through a field with a hedge right. Go through a gate at the top of the field and in the next field stay right again to reach another gate. Now with a wall on the right the path passes above a farm and through a gate the path reaches a track. Turn right on to the track to go steeply uphill to reach a road.

Turn left to walk along the road into Bolsterstone village to reach a junction with the village hall in front. Go right, and then immediate left on to Heads Lane which passes to the right of the hall. After half a mile take note of a path on the left which leads to a farm down below which the route passes through on the way back. The lane carries on climbing gently, shortly becoming more of a track as it passes through a gate just after the last house is passed. Still climbing, after a further third of a mile, where a path meets the track from the right, the track heads off downhill to the left. Go off the track here to go straight forward on to a grassy area at the start of Whitwell Moor and head for the trig point up ahead on the left.

After admiring the views from the trig point go half right towards trees going through any of the gaps in a broken wall on to a path which carries on in the same direction, staying to the right of the trees. Just before the path reaches a road, double back left on a path into the woods. The path here isn't clear but to start with for about 200 yards it runs parallel to the previous path before it drops down to the bottom of the woods to a wall.

At the wall corner there is a gap in the wall. Go through it, and ignoring a path right, go straight forwards on to an enclosed green lane. The lane leaves the woods to go through farmland with fields on both sides. Further on the lane becomes a track and passes 2 farms on the right before bending left to go uphill. At the top of the hill the track is back at the cross paths from earlier. Turn right here and after just under a mile take the path right to go through the farm down below. Carry on downhill through 2 fields with a wall to the left before the path leaves the wall to cross the field to enter a wood.

After 200 yards take a path right which goes down 2 sets of steps then tracks the road for about 400 yards before bending left to come out on to the road. Turn right to walk along the road for a few yards, then after crossing a bridge take a path left which stays between the road and Broomhead reservoir for ¾ of a mile before coming out on to the road at a small parking area. Here, take a path to the left which carries on in the same direction with the reservoir still on the left for just over half a mile to reach a road. Cross the road on to a path opposite, which stays alongside More Hall reservoir for a mile to reach the dam wall. Turn left here to walk along the dam wall to return to the start.

Look out for…..

Bolsterstone Castle, but you'll never find it! Bolsterstone has a Castle Inn, Castle Cottage, Castle Farm, Castle Garth and Castle Green, but there's no castle. A few years ago, Bolsterstone Castle Project got a £20,000 grant to investigate and after excavations, remains of 15th and 16th century buildings, possibly a large manor house were found, but no signs of a castle.

Bolster Stones. There is a theory that the village gets its name from two large stones which can be found in the local church yard. The two stones possibly formed the base for twin Anglo Saxon Crosses … others think they were the base from a local Gibbet.

Dog Suitability

Dogs can be off-lead for all of this walk apart from the road sections, and when passing through the farm.

Refreshments

Food and drink can be obtained at the Castle Inn at Bolsterstone.

Walk No 28 : Moorseats Hall

4 miles / 2 hours

Introduction

This is a Peak District walk in the Hathersage area which starts off within the Sheffield city boundary, but for the most part takes place in Derbyshire. Starting from Upper Burbage bridge the route heads off along Fiddlers Elbow towards Higgar Tor before breaking away across Callow Bank to the Outseats area of Hathersage. Some road walking and farm tracks then lead to Moorseats Hall, tucked away in the shelter of Carhead Rocks. Leaving Moorseats, after crossing Cattis-side Moor on the way up to Stanage Edge, some boulder hopping is needed to return to the start. There are some great views of the Hope Valley from the top of Stanage, and also of Hathersage on the paths leading to Moorseats, and from further up the hill approaching Cattis-side. This is another walk which is good for keen photographers!

Hathersage gate on the way to Moorseats Hall

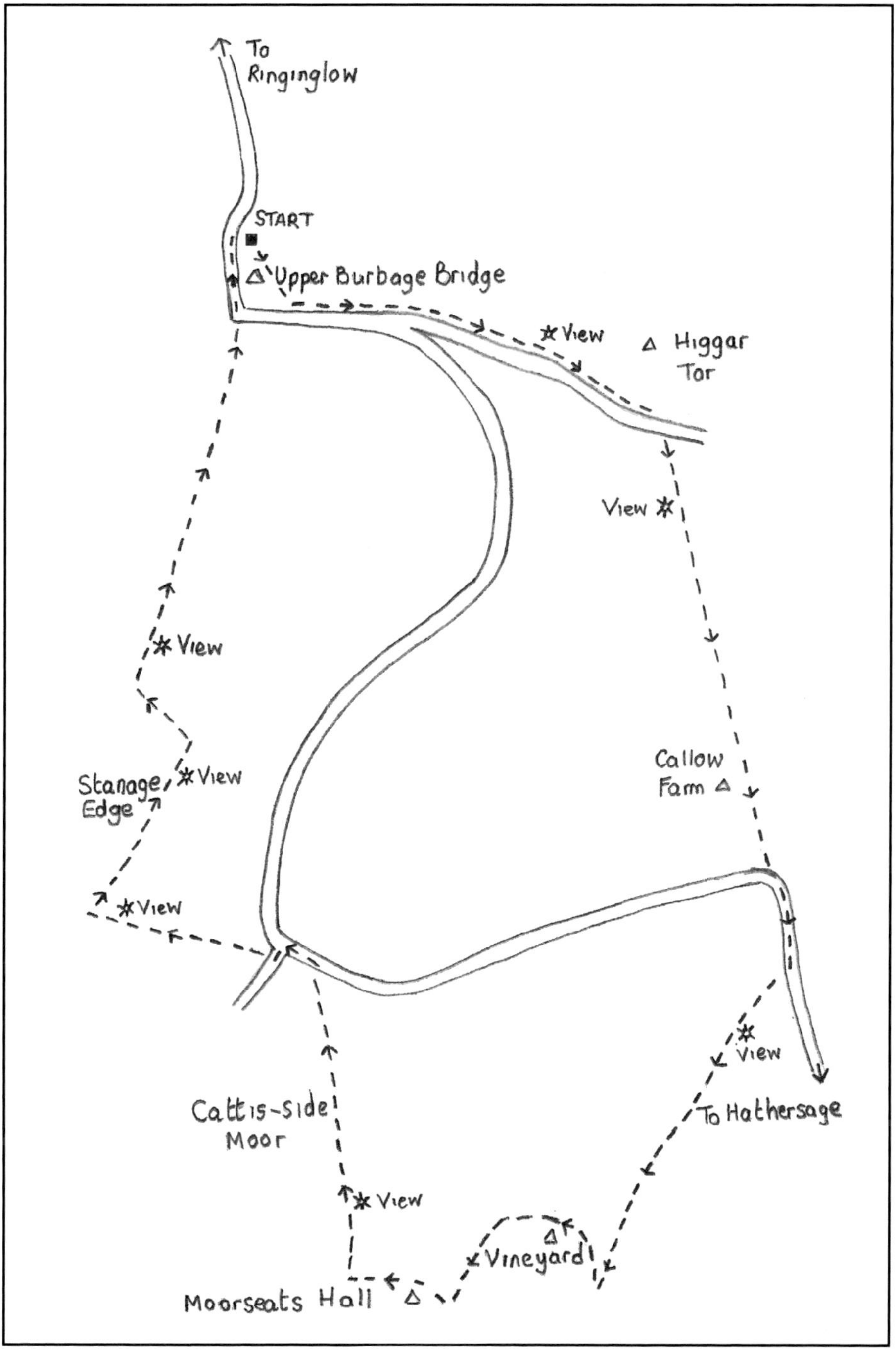

To Ringinglow
START
Upper Burbage Bridge
View
Higgar Tor
View
View
Stanage Edge
View
View
Callow Farm
View
To Hathersage
Cattis-side Moor
View
Vineyard
Moorseats Hall

Walk Difficulty

This is not an easy walk, it having three climbs in total, one of which is quite strenuous, and another one which involves a short climb through rocks. There is also a couple of tricky downhill sections, and at certain times of year there can be quite a lot of mud and standing water.

Starting Point

Upper Burbage Bridge car park on Ringinglow Road, Sheffield, S32 1BR. What3words: **stocks.manage.bulb**

The Route

Facing uphill, go through a gate to the left then turn immediate right to walk alongside a wire fence on a path which stays close to the road as it heads towards Higgar Tor. After half a mile a signpost is reached for a path leading left towards Higgar Tor. Ignore this path to go through the gate on the right to cross the road, and then go back up the road for about 20 yards to go through a gate on the left. Through the gate, take an immediate path going half left, which after a while drops steeply downhill on a grassy path which can be very slippery. After 3/4 of a mile the renovated Callow Farm building is passed on the right before the path comes out on to a road. Turn left to walk down the road for about 250 yards, then turn right at a signpost to go through a gate on to a track leading uphill. As views of Hathersage open up to the left, go through a gate with 'Hathersage' on it on the left, just before a farm.

After going through a second gate the path goes half left downhill to the far right corner. Into the next field the path stays next to trees on the right, then at the bottom the path leads down to a tarmacced drive. Turn right to walk up the drive and stay on it as it bends left, crossing a cattle grid to reach the entrance to Moorseats Hall. At this point it is hard to believe that the driveway which passes the house is a public right of way, but it is, and after going through the gateway, stay on the drive as it bends right and then left on its way steeply uphill. At the top of the hill, the drive bends right, and just after passing a corrugated house on the right, go through a gate on the left on to an access path across moorland. The path carries on climbing steeply for a while before levelling off as Stanage Edge comes into view. When the path reaches a road, turn left, and then at the junction, go left again.

Pass through parked cars on the right to find a clear path leading up to the top of Stanage Edge. Once at the top turn right to walk close to the Edge, and head towards the trig point. After taking in the views, turn left here, on to a path which steadily drops down through rocks. To the right in the far distance can be seen the car park where the walk started, and a path cutting through the heather to reach it. There are several ways through the rocks on the right to get to this path. The first involves climbing down through rocks, but a better option is an easier path which to start with leads away from the path below, but soon bends right to get on to it, at the bottom of the edge. Once on this path stay on it all the way to the road, then carry on in the same direction to reach the car park.

Look out for…..

Callow Farm. In 1770, a former owner of the farm, George Fox built the nearby Fox House pub and named it after himself. The farm was ruined in the 1970's and in 2021 work commenced to restore the building.

Hope Valley Vineyard situated 900 feet above sea level is the highest vineyard in the country. It covers 1.5 acres at Carr Head Farm and currently produces a sparkling rosé, a still rosé and a still white. It was created in 2017 as a retirement project by the owners of the farm.

Moorseats Hall dates back to the 1300s. The mansion once had a famous house guest, Charlotte Brontë, who used the hall as an inspiration for her book Jane Eyre. She named the heroine of the novel after the owners of the hall and a Moor House also features prominently in the book.

Stanage Edge was used in the 2005 remake of Pride and Prejudice. Stanage and the North Lees Estate were once private grouse moors and gamekeepers were often bribed to allow access to rock climbers in the 19th century.

Dog Suitability

Dogs will need to be kept under close control throughout the walk because of sheep in the fields and on the moors. At Springtime the area around Stanage is a breeding ground for ring ouzels so special care needs to be taken then.

Refreshments

There is a choice of pubs and cafes close by in the village of Hathersage.

Walk No 29 : Crook Hill

8.5 miles / 4.5 hours

Introduction

This is a walk in the Ladybower area which has fabulous views throughout the walk, and a great variety of scenery along the way too. The walk starts from the Ashopton Viaduct with a stiff climb up Crook Hill before crossing fields to Lockerbrook and a great view back down the valley. This is followed by a descent down to Derwent Reservoir to reach the halfway point. From there, the return route is more gentle, which following a visit to Fairholmes Visitors Centre, takes place along lanes across the far side of Ladybower reservoir. Here, the remains of Derwent, one of the two villages flooded in the creation of the Ladybower can be seen, unlike the other village Ashopton, which lies beneath Ashopton Viaduct, never to be seen again.

Crook Hill, as seen from Ashopton Bridge

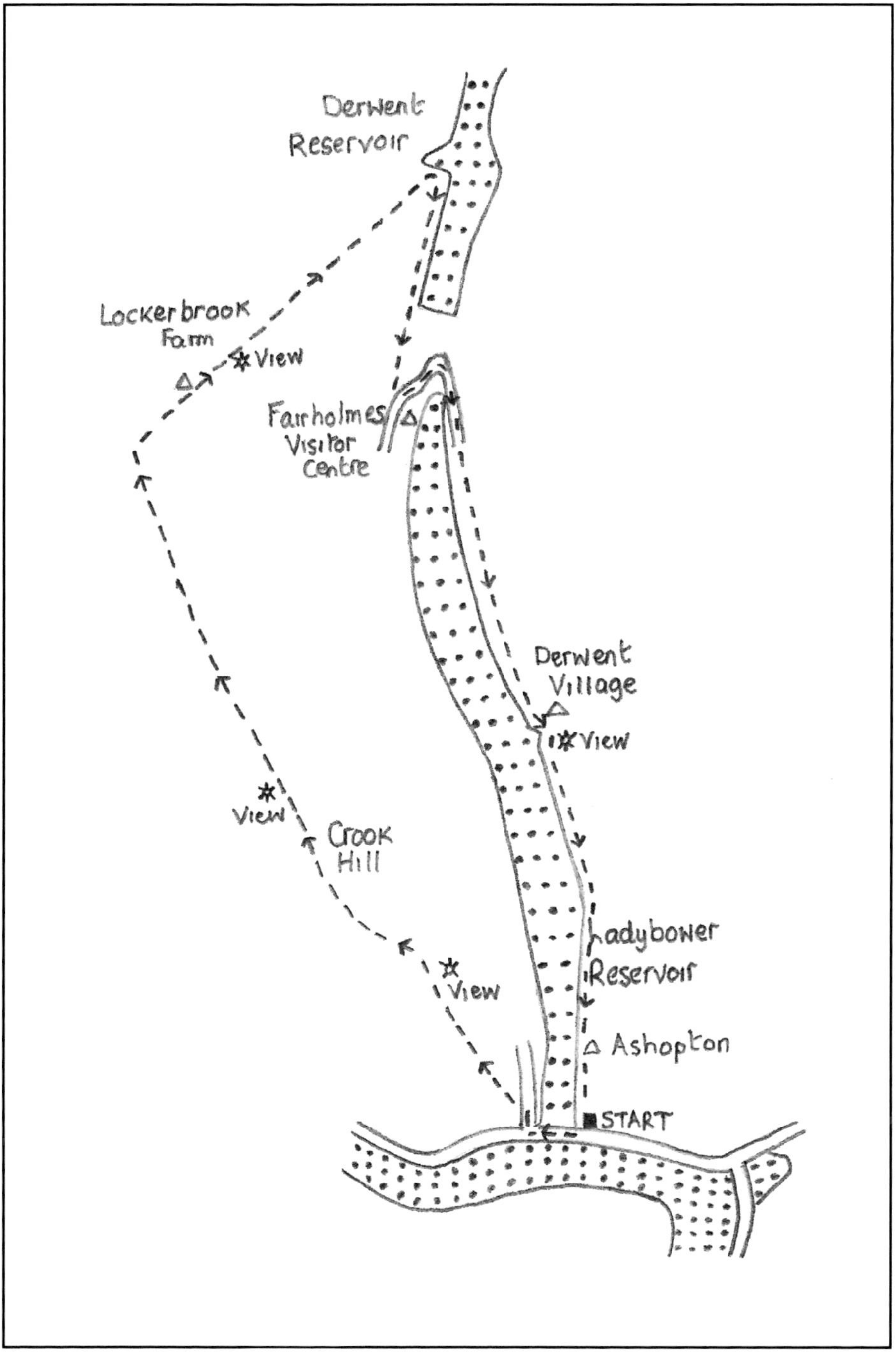
Derwent
Reservoir
Lockerbrook
Farm
View
Fairholmes
Visitor
Centre
Derwent
Village
View
View
Crook
Hill
Ladybower
Reservoir
View
Ashopton
START

Walk Difficulty

After the initial climb, this is not too difficult a walk, and takes place on fairly good paths although some of them can have standing water, and be muddy in winter, and after heavy rain.

Starting Point

The car parking area on the A57 just before Ashopton Bridge, situated just through the traffic lights at the Ladybower Reservoir coming from the Sheffield direction. No postcode for the parking area, but What3Words are **fake.idea.verve.** If the parking area is full, Heatherdene Car Park on Ashopton Road (A6013) is close by. What3Words: **kettles.hoops.warned**

The Route

From the car parking area, cross the road and turn left to walk over Ashopton Bridge. Across the bridge turn right to walk along the side road for about 30 yards, then cross the road to climb steps to go through a gate into a field. Up the hill the path soon bends right to head towards a gate in the top right corner. With a farm in front, go through the gate and go right to reach another gate. Through this gate the path carries on uphill and stays to the left of the field, to reach a gate in the top left corner, next to farm buildings.

Go through the gate to cross a farm track and then through another gate on the other site of the track. In the next field the path goes half right to head up to a wall in the top right corner. Through another gate, there are three tracks next to each other, all leading to the right. Take the middle one which soon bends to the left and heads towards the top left corner of a wall in the distance. At this point there are a number of paths which can be taken, going in every direction, and it can be quite confusing. However, there is a good marker point to bear in mind, which is the large conifer plantation ahead in the distance, which is what the route eventually reaches. Going back to the instructions, at the wall mentioned previously, take a path at the other side of the wall which keeps the wall to the right of it to start with. Through two gates the path goes half left on an obvious path which climbs a field. The path now crosses three more fields, keeping in the same direction, with the plantation getting ever nearer.

On reaching the plantation, the path carries on to the left of the trees and stays there for almost a mile, passing through two gates at one point, but still keeping in the same direction. Where the plantation ends, there are a number of paths leading off in different directions, and for our route, take one of the two choices for turning right. Either can be taken, as long as the plantation is still kept to the right. The path is now a track, the reason for this being that it leads to cottages and the Outdoor Centre at Lockerbrook Farm. This is passed after about five minutes or so of walking, and it may be of interest to note that just after the farm, after going through a gate, that there are a few steps on the left which at the top of is a perfect spot to have a coffee stop, looking down at the Derwent Valley and Ladybower Reservoir down below in the distance.

Back on the path, carry on straight forward, ignoring any paths to the right signposted for Fairholmes or Derwent to enter woods after about half a mile. From here, the path starts to descend towards the Derwent Reservoir, gently to start with, then quite steeply further down. After just under a mile the path reaches the reservoir. Turn right here on to a road which leads to Fairholmes Visitors Centre where there are toilet facilities, refreshments and a picnic area.

From the picnic area in front of the Visitors Centre, and facing the reservoir, take a path left which leads downhill to join a road further down which to start with heads towards the Derwent Dam wall. It soon veers right though and leads to the other side of Ladybower. This is Derwent Lane which passes a number of houses and an old school as it makes its way to the site of the flooded Derwent village on the right of the lane. With a few bends along the way, the lane stays in roughly the same direction alongside Ladybower reservoir for just over two and a half miles to return to the start.

Look out for…..

Lockerbrook Farm Outdoor Centre which was created by volunteers from Sheffield Woodcraft Folk in 1964 to provide a place for young people from inner cities to have an opportunity to develop the skills and knowledge to be confident in the outdoors. Lockerbrook comprises of a bunk barn sleeping up to 36, and a cottage sleeping six.

Derwent Village. Although it was smaller than Ashopton, Derwent had both Catholic and Anglican churches and an impressive manor house. It was demolished in 1943, except for the church steeple which stood defiantly out of the waters for some time before it to was dynamited in 1947 (for safety reasons!). The village was drowned in 1944 and has mostly stayed hidden under the dark waters ever since. In the dry summers of 1976, 1995 and 2018 the remains of the village surfaced for all to see.

Ashopton Village. The main part of Ashopton village sat under where the viaduct carries the A57 across the reservoir, and whereas the remains of Derwent are visible when the water levels are low, Ashopton will never be seen again as silt has covered the remains of the buildings. When it was destroyed Ashopton had a population of around 100 people. Records show that in 1829, the village hosted a wool fair, a tradition that took place annually in July. Ashopton also had a village inn, post office, a hall and a chapel.

Dog Suitability

To start with on the climb up Crook Hill dogs will need to be led, but after that, apart from the road walking, dogs can be off-lead most of the way.

Refreshments

There is a takeaway kiosk at Fairholmes Visitors Centre for food and drink, and the Ladybower Inn is close to the parking area as well.

Walk No 30 : Ughill Moor

4.5 miles / 2.25 hours

Introduction

This is another Sheffield walk which takes place entirely within the Peak District, and enjoys amazing views across the moors from start to finish. In a quiet area high above both the Loxley and Rivelin valleys, the route uses little-used paths and tracks to cross Ughill Moor, and open countryside nearby. There is a real feeling of history at the start of the walk as an old packhorse route across the moor is taken within minutes of leaving the parking area, very soon to be followed by outstanding views across to the Dale Dike reservoir and Bradfield village in the distance. Following a short road section in the Ughill area, farm tracks, a moorland path and another road section are used to return to the start.

Looking back towards Shepherd Heights from Platts Farm

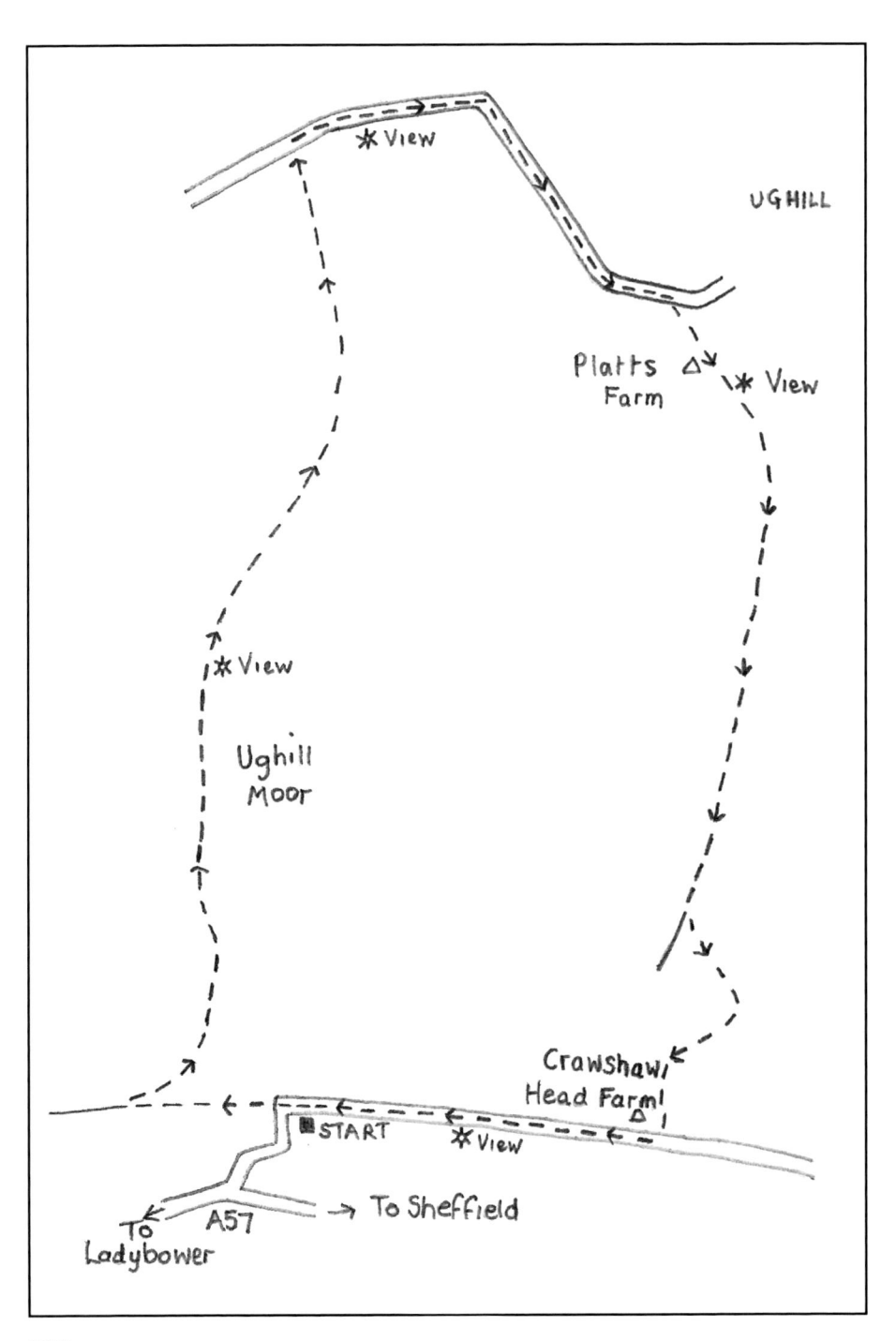

Walk Difficulty

Although the paths are pretty good throughout, there is the usual possibility of mud on the moorland section in winter and after heavy rain.

Starting Point

There is a small parking area on a road called Rod Side at Hollow Meadows. There is no postcode for the meeting place, but it can be found by taking the A57 Manchester Road away from Sheffield towards the Ladybower, then turning right 200 yards after Centre Barks (S6 6GL) on to Rod Side. The parking area can be found after 500 yards, on the 2nd right bend. What3Words: **blocks.modes.still**

The Route

From the roadside parking, turn left along the road for a few yards, and where the road bends left carry on straight forwards on to a track. After a few yards the track reaches a gate. After passing through the gate turn right on to a minor path alongside a fence to reach another gate about 40 yards away. Go through the gate on to an old packhorse route, Stake Hill Road and stay on this mostly enclosed track for 1.5 miles until it reaches a road. Turn right on the road and stay on it as it bends right to go downhill.

At the bottom of the hill the road levels and bends left to quickly reach a road junction. Take the right turn here which looks like a farm drive but is also a public footpath. This is another old packhorse route, Platts Lane. After passing Platts Farm the lane carries on for 0.75 miles to approach Crawshaw Farm. Just before the farm there is a house on the left with a footpath just before it which heads across a field passing to the left of the farm.

At a gate go over a stile next to it which leads back on to Platts Lane. Cross over the lane on to a narrow path opposite as the route now crosses Ughill Moor. The path here cuts diagonally right to climb up through moorland until at its highest point it bends left to head towards a road. This moorland path isn't always very clear once it reaches the top section, but a good landmark is Crawshaw Head Farm which can be seen in the distance, on the right.

By keeping the same distance from Crawshaw Head Farm a route through the heather can be found to reach the road half a mile after leaving Platts Lane. Go over a wall stile where the moor meets the road, then turn right to walk along the road for just over half a mile to return to the start.

Look out for…..

Platts Farm has been home to many historical figures including the Earl of Shrewsbury, Bess of Hardwick and the Duke of Norfolk. It was also used as an alehouse during the 17th century, before being converted to a farm with two adjoining cottages in the 19th century.

Ughill is a tiny hamlet which was mentioned in the Domesday Book but was established before this by Norwegian Vikings in the 10th century. Ughill Hall is most famous for a double murder in 1986. Ian Wood shot and killed his mistress and her daughter and then went on the run. Eight days later he surrendered to authorities in France after threatening to commit suicide by jumping off Amiens Cathedral.

Crawshaw Head Farm. In 1876 George Helliwell of Crawshaw Head was prosecuted under the 1860 Adulteration Act which was used to prosecute food suppliers who *"added or subtracted any substance to or from food so that the natural composition and quality of the food is affected"*. It seems that George's milk was deemed to be sub-standard, and a prosecution was taken out against him. Fortunately for George though, the prosecution failed, due to a problem with the Town Clerk accidently getting milk samples mixed up, and the tested one produced in court being passed as sound, putting George in the clear. The Town Clerk had to apologise for the maladministration, and the case against George was dismissed. Four years later George liquidated his business at Crawshaw Head, with debts of £850.

Dog Suitability

As there are sheep throughout the route, dogs will need to be kept under close control at all times.

Refreshments

The simple advice for this walk is to take your own refreshments as the nearest places to obtain food or drink are pubs at Dungworth and Ladybower, both about three miles away.

BEECHES
of WALKLEY

A *family run inner city farm shop*

We are passionate about local food produce

Fresh Meat, Fruit, Local Ales & Sundries

Scoop your own frozen fruit and veg

Come try our award winning sausages

Opening hours
8am – 6pm Monday – Saturday

290 - 296 South Road Walkley Sheffield S6 3TE
tel: 0114 2313018 / 0114 2340066 tw. @BeechesWalkley

Sheffield and Peak District Walking Group

All the walks in this book are walks that have been put together for our walking group. Altogether we have over 130 walks and are still adding to the total to make sure that we're not forever repeating the same ones. Although some of the walks we do are only 4 miles long, there are very few of the walks which don't have some type of challenge in them. Whether this is a steep hill, lots of stiles, muddy paths or rocky sections varies from walk to walk. One thing we like to do though is not rush, and make sure that we enjoy our surroundings as we walk along.

New members are always welcome, but we do ask that when people come on the walks that they wear adequate clothing and footwear, and bring sufficient food and drink for the duration of the walks. We are currently arranging on average 2 walks a week all year round and below are details of what to expect on our walks.

Morning walks – at the moment these are taking place on Fridays and Saturdays, usually twice a month on both days. They are normally 4-5 miles long, and last 2 – 2.5 hours. The usual meet up time is 9 o clock..

Sunday walks – these are full day walks and again we normally meet around 9 o clock. The walks usually take between 4 and 5.5 hours and are 7-10 miles long. Experienced walkers are most suited to these walks.

Evening walks – are either sunset, twilight or torch walks depending on the time of year! At the moment these walks take place on Tuesday nights in summer daylight hours.

How to find out about the walks: The walks are advertised through a newsletter which is emailed out to people who have subscribed to it. To be added to the mailing list email **sheffieldandpeakdistrictwalks@gmail.com**. There is also a Facebook page which can be found by searching for Sheffield and Peak District walks.

The Countryside Code

Respect other people
- Consider the local community and other people enjoying the outdoors
- Park carefully so access to gateways and driveways is clear
- Leave gates and property as you find them
- Follow paths but give way to others where it's narrow

Protect the natural environment
- Leave no trace of your visit, take all your litter home
- Don't have BBQs or fires
- Keep dogs under effective control
- Dog poo - bag it and bin it

Enjoy the outdoors
- Plan ahead, check what facilities are open, be prepared
- Follow advice and local signs and obey social distancing measures

Enjoy, be safe

About the Author

Steve lives in the North of Sheffield where he has lived all his life. His passion for walking started as a boy when in his own words "we used to walk everywhere", including long Sunday family walks. For most of his adult life he has been a dog owner, and taking his dogs for long walks, and also enjoying walking with his family as he was growing up prepared him for the more serious walking which he has enjoyed with walking groups since 2006. For the last two years, with Andrea's help, he has branched out to run his own walking group, the Sheffield and Peak District Walking Group, which is where the name for his books has come from. After working in the Motor Trade for most of his working life, prior to semi-retirement, Steve became a self-taught painter and decorator whilst managing to fit several walks a week in as a professional walking guide. Nowadays, he is happy to devote all his time to leading walks, and writing and selling books!